MOON WISE

The World's Mysterious Companion

It would be hard to find an object that means more things to more people than the Moon. It is a rocky satellite, a spur to madness, or a goddess—to name a few. Nothing has fired our collective imagination and quest for knowledge more than this perennial, ever-changing ruler of the night sky.

This book will take you on a journey of discovery about the invisible effects of the Moon on our inner and outer worlds. From tides to tirades, from planting to pleasure, see how the lunar influence triggers a myriad of effects.

If you like to read your horoscope, then you already know about your Sun sign. *Moon Wise* lets you find out about the other half—your Moon sign. Discover how the Moon affects you emotionally, physically, and mentally as it makes its monthly journey through the signs of the Zodiac.

About the Author

Born and raised in America's Desert Southwest, Daniel Pharr knew his path was Pagan after he first was introduced to the ways of the Goddess more than twenty years ago. He has studied the ancient arts of healing, divination, astrology, and the magical uses of herbs. Daniel is a certified firewalk instructor and a teacher of martial arts with a black belt in Kenpo karate. His private practice extends to organizations and corporations as well as individuals. Today he resides in the Pacific Northwest with his dog Kevin.

To Write to the Author

If you wish to contact the author or would like more information about this book, please write to the author in care of Llewellyn Worldwide and we will forward your request. Both the author and publisher appreciate hearing from you and learning of your enjoyment of this book and how it has helped you. Llewellyn Worldwide cannot guarantee that every letter written to the author can be answered, but all will be forwarded. Please write to:

Daniel Pharr
℅ Llewellyn Worldwide
P.O. Box 64383, Dept. K521–5
St. Paul, MN 55164-0383, U.S.A.

Please enclose a self-addressed stamped envelope for reply, or $1.00 to cover costs. If outside U.S.A., enclose international postal reply coupon.

DANIEL PHARR

MOON WISE

Astrology, Self-Understanding and Lunar Energies

2000
Llewellyn Publications
St. Paul, Minnesota 55164-0383, U.S.A.

First Edition
First Printing, 2000

Cover design by Anne Marie Garrison
Book design and editing by Eila Savela
Author photograph by Ariel M. Frager

Library of Congress Cataloging-in-Publication Data
(Pending)

Llewellyn Worldwide does not participate in, endorse, or have any authority or responsibility concerning private business transactions between our authors and the public.

All mail addressed to the author is forwarded but the publisher cannot, unless specifically instructed by the author, give out an address or phone number.

Llewellyn Publications
A Division of Llewellyn Worldwide, Ltd.
P.O. Box 64383, Dept. K521–5
St. Paul, MN 55164-0383, U.S.A.
www.llewellyn.com

Printed in the United States of America

Dedication

This book is dedicated to my children, Jimmy and Amber.

Personal Thanks

To my sweet friend, Ariel.

Through you, I have seen a world that eluded me for many years. Your artistic expression of life inspires me to create and master my craft. Thank you for your gifts of love and support.

Contents

Preface

Years ago, I left my teacher's apprenticeship armed with a power that reshaped my life—the power of the Moon. The Moon's pull is so great that it causes ocean tides and changes weather patterns. The Moon also affects emotions.

Before I discovered the power of the Moon, I suppressed my emotions as I thought all men did. Although I appeared to be calm and self-assured, I was also scared. I had emotions and emotional reactions, but refused to let them out except in private fits of tears and rage. The harder I worked to suppress these emotions, the more difficult they became.

My studies sensitized me to the Moon's energies, and I discovered something that changed my life. There was a relationship between the astrological position of the Moon and my emotions. When the Moon was in Cancer, I cried. Absolutely everything upset me, especially relationships. When the Moon was in Aries, I argued with everyone. My fuse was short, and I angered quickly.

My continued research indicated these were not the only two Moon signs that affected me. Each Moon had a different influence: happy, analytical, motivated, talkative, or sexy. I became fascinated with this phenomenon. By tracking my feelings and comparing them to the Moon, I found patterns that allowed me to predict which days of the month would be the most challenging or the most rewarding. In time, my emotional swings began to mellow because I was aware of the Moon's influence and chose to deal with my emotions rather than to be their victim.

I discovered other uses for my lunar lessons. I realized that the Moon affected everybody in a similar fashion. I could predict how people would react to a given situation. Suddenly, I was able to choose the right day to ask for a raise or a vacation. I knew when to negotiate for a new car and when not to negotiate for a house. I discovered some days are better for communicating and giving presentations, and other days are best spent alone.

Through the power of the Moon I learned about myself and other people. I was surprised to find we are much more similar than we are different. I was becoming less scared of what other people thought of me, because they were like me. They had the same emotional reactions I did. It became safe for me to express my feelings. When I openly discussed my feelings, the people around me would share their feelings. This created intimacy, and I found some lifelong friends. I also learned what intimacy means in a relationship and how to promote it. Since then, I have become successful at maintaining a loving and caring relationship.

This book is about self-discovery. It will help you understand the Moon's cycles and teach you to take advantage of the Moon's power. You will learn to predict your emotional reactions and the reactions of others.

Each of the twelve Moon signs has a different effect. Some influence you to be happy, while others cause you to be angry. Some help you to exaggerate the truth, while others act like lie detectors. Each is a teacher. From these Moons you will learn who you are, why you do what you do, and how to quickly improve every relationship in your life.

Chapter 1

The Moon

Life on Earth is dramatically influenced by the Moon. Legends tell of werewolves and lunatics. Urban myths attribute much to the Moon: drunkenness, disorderly conduct, and murders. Evidence from our physical world substantiates the Moon's influence.

For centuries, it has been believed that the Moon affects the weather. Llewellyn's *Moon Sign Book* gives several examples. It is said if the Moon becomes full near midnight, the next seven days will enjoy good weather. If the full Moon occurs at noon, the weather will be unpredictable. A ring around the Moon indicates the coming of rain, while the same ring at moonrise indicates heavy rain.

Pale Moon doth rain, red Moon doth blow, white Moon doth neither rain or snow.

Ring around the Moon, rain coming soon.

When 'round the Moon there is a brugh, the weather will be cold and rough.

Clear Moon, frost soon.

For an indication of good weather to come, the new Moon should cast a shadow within four days. If no shadow is cast from the Moon for four days, foul weather will follow. A dusky lower horn of the crescent Moon indicates rain before the full Moon. In contrast, sharp horns on the third day of the crescent Moon foretells good weather all month. A misty upper horn at moonset brings rain before the new Moon, and if the center of the Moon is hazy, the full Moon will be rainy.

In a month with two full Moons, the second, known as a "blue" Moon, will likely bring severe weather, especially in May. A vernal equinox full Moon foretells flooding followed by an abnormally dry season. Stormy weather quickly follows a full Moon at the spring equinox, but overall, the spring will be dry.

Studies show monthly weather patterns mimic the lunar cycle. In *Supernature*, Lyall Watson discusses two independent studies conducted in the 1960s on the Moon's effect on rainfall. The Australian study looked at weather patterns over a period of twenty-five years. The American-based study examined forty-nine years of weather history. Both found rainfall increases in the days following new and full Moons. Each study presented the same conclusion: there is a connection between the Moon's monthly cycles and regular rainfall patterns.

Research has also shown ice formation in high clouds and the concentration of ozone in the atmosphere follows the Moon's lunations. The magnetic field surrounding the earth fluctuates in patterns similar to the lunar cycle. The *Journal of Geophysical Research* published weather studies in the 1960s confirming a number of natural phenomena cycling in concert with the Moon. These lunar patterns were found in the ozone concentration in the atmosphere, the quantity of ice particles in high altitude clouds, the heaviest rainfall in the United States and New Zealand, fluctuations in the earth's magnetic field, and the number of meteors falling into the earth's atmosphere.

There are many tales and beliefs which relate the keeping of animals to the phases of the Moon. Hamsters were found to be more active immediately after new Moons and full Moons in a four-year study cited by Watson in *Supernature*. Zookeepers can show the mating cycles of their keep to be in conjunction with lunar cycles. Sooty terns, which are inhabitants of the Ascension Islands, are known as "wide-awakes" because they only mate at night. The sooty tern breeds every tenth full Moon and only every tenth full Moon.

The most visible lunar effects are ocean tides. Consequently, animals that are normally part of the tidal ecosystem are affected by the Moon's changes. This is only natural because the tidal waters are just that—ocean water moving in lunar cycles. These studies show that tidal creatures, if taken from their normal habitat to a location hundreds of miles inland, adapt themselves to what would be the tidal cycles if their new home had a coastline. This was proven with oysters even when kept in containers and not exposed to sunlight or moonlight. Grunion (a small fish that lives off the coastal waters of California and Mexico) are at some level aware of the increased height of spring tides. On or just after the full Moon, when the spring tides are about to recede, the grunion lay their eggs above the high tide line. There the eggs incubate until the next spring high tide, when the young hatch and swim into the tide.

Natives of tidal waters aren't the only creatures that react to the Moon's changes. As a scuba instructor, I've observed underwater life to be more active during the full Moon, and encountered many more sharks, barracudas, rays, and moray eels under the shining orb. A six-foot sand shark swam within arm's length of me during a night dive off the coast of Bimini Island in the Bahamas. Its predatory, erratic movements indicated that the shark was foraging. Underwater flashlights only punch a short beam of light through the water, which greatly limits visibility, but that night the ocean glowed with an eerie luminescence from the light of the full Moon. Spotting the shadowy figure set against the penetrating lunar light allowed time to compose myself and prepare for the shark's arrival rather than panicking when this man-sized creature bolted through my flashlight's beam.

In pre-Christian times, our ancestors were hunters and gatherers. As our ancestors began to farm, they became more dependent on the weather. Previously, severe weather inhibited the hunt; as farmers, severe weather could ruin an entire year's crop. They began to take notice of nature's cycles and adapted their old rituals to their current existence. Birth, life, and death were honored. The power of the feminine became obvious as they related their own birth experiences to that of animals and plants.

They learned from watching the patterns around them and the reactions of other living creatures. Many "old wives' tales" have their basis in fact. In the time before Christianity, people lived in conjunction with nature's seasonal changes. They planted and harvested by the solar and lunar clocks, and foretold the weather by observing nature's signs. When the lives of pre-Christian people are examined, their belief in the connection of the Moon with fertility and farming is apparent. The connection between solar and lunar cycles and farming continues to this day.

Solar planting provides the basis for most of the agricultural season. Ground preparation begins around the spring (or vernal) equinox. This is also the season for pruning. Cultivation and the first plantings begin at the vernal equinox and continue through Beltaine. Early harvesting begins at the summer solstice, while planting continues. Honey is gathered. The first real harvest is at Lammas and is celebrated as Thanksgiving. The second harvest is at the autumnal equinox, and the last is at Hallows. Crop remains after harvest are turned under, allowing the earth to reabsorb that which sprang from it. Herbs, onions, garlic, and chilies are hung to dry. Seeds are collected for the next year's spring planting.

Lunar gardening is based upon planting, weeding, and harvesting during different phases of the Moon. These activities are also coordinated with the Moon signs. Plantings generally do best when planted in the first, second, or third quarters of the Moon, with each quarter being more conducive to some plants than others. Weeding and cultivation are best accomplished in the Moon's fourth quarter. Water signs (Cancer, Scorpio, and Pisces) are the best times for planting and irrigation. The Fire Moons (Aries, Leo, and Sagittarius) are used for weeding and the elimination of pests.

Plant life responds to changes in the Moon. There are hundreds of tales and beliefs regarding planting and harvesting. Some portions of the lunar month are better for planting than others, while some are better for harvesting. Harvesting plants for food has different lunar requirements than harvesting the same plants for medicinal purposes.

Almanacs based on the lunar cycle have helped farmers plan on the weather and on the growth cycle of plants for centuries. The *Old Farmer's Almanac* was established in 1792 by its founder, Robert B. Thomas (1766-1846), and is the "oldest continually published periodical in North America." It contains stories on all aspects of life, as well as numerous charts and indices containing astronomical conjunctions, astrological Moon placements, and tide tables, to name a few.

Experiments have been conducted to determine the validity of claims about Moon gardening. As discussed in *Llewellyn's 1994 Organic Gardening Almanac,* Dr. Clark Timmins conducted tests in which the Moon's sign was the only planting indicator. Initially the phases of the Moon were not taken into account. He found that beets sown in a Scorpio Moon had a germination rate of 71 percent, while 58 percent of those sown in a Sagittarius Moon germinated. Marigolds sown in a Cancer Moon had a germination rate of 90 percent, in comparison to a 32 percent rate under a Leo Moon. Dr. Timmins also found that tomatoes planted during the Cancer Moon had a germination rate of 90 percent, compared to tomatoes planted during a Leo Moon, which only germinated 58 percent of the time.

Additional experimentation included the Moon's phases in different Moon signs. One test involved the transplantation of tomato seedlings during a waxing Cancer Moon and a waning Sagittarius Moon. The results were a 100 percent survival rate during the waxing Cancer Moon and a 100 percent mortality rate for the seedlings transplanted during the waning Sagittarius Moon.

The testing conducted also addressed the size of the plants and of the yield. Plants sown in a Cancer Moon had blossoms twelve days before those planted in Leo. The Cancer-sown plants were also considerably larger, produced harvestable fruit sooner, and yielded substantially larger fruit than the Leo-sown plants.

The phases of the Moon, in regard to farming, are basically split into two: increasing or waxing, and decreasing or waning. Generally, crops grown aboveground should be planted during a waxing Moon and crops grown underground should be planted during the waning Moon. *Llewellyn's 1994 Organic Gardening Almanac* recommends planting by lunar quarters. During the first quarter plant leafy, aboveground annuals that produce seeds outside the fruit; in the second quarter plant viny, aboveground annuals that produce seeds inside the fruit, except cucumbers, which do best in the first quarter. In the third quarter plant biennials, perennials, bulbs, and root plants such as trees, shrubs, berries, beets, carrots, onions, and potatoes. Reserve the fourth quarter for weeding and cultivating.

Studies conducted since World War II that link the Moon's metamorphosis to the body's illnesses and functions demonstrate our amazing lunar connection. In the 1940s, deaths from tuberculosis would peak one week prior to the full Moon. This is explained by a connection between the blood pH and phases of the Moon. In *Many Moons,* Diana Brueton indicates a similar theory exists for pneumonia.

There have been studies that show that bleeding from operations is considerably more intense during or around the time of the full Moon. Watson, in *Supernature,* states that Dr. Edson Andrews, an American researcher, found 82 percent of surgical bleeding problems were in the second and third lunar quarters with a significant increase on the full Moon.

Studies have shown a correlation between migraine headaches and the new and full Moons. Migraine affliction patterns have also been found to match women's menstrual cycles. Lucy, an astrologer friend, is very susceptible to migraine headaches and gets one in conjunction with every full Moon.

Folklore describes women becoming pregnant by the full Moon, and the Moon herself having a menstrual cycle. Although we know this isn't true, a woman's menstrual cycle is of approximately the same duration as one lunation. Studies indicate a woman's menstrual cycle is often timed in conjunction with lunar cycles, and many women menstruate during a new or full Moon.

There is also a documented rise in birth rates during the new and full Moons. A rise in birth rates on or around the full Moon was documented by Tallahassee Memorial Hospital in the 1950s. They found a remarkable increase in births at the full Moon. A correlation was found between the lunar cycle and the birth rate in New York City, where 510,000 births were studied between 1948 and 1958. According to Diana Brueton in *Many Moons*, two independent German studies found a correlation in the birth rate and the high tide.

Man has blamed his shortcomings on the Moon for centuries. The whole gambit of emotional behavior and misbehavior has been the Moon's fault, from crying at a movie, to driving erratically, to fighting, drunkenness, and even rape and murder.

The full Moon makes everyone just a little bit crazy. We become "lunatics." This connection between the Moon and lunacy is one of the most widely discussed phenomena related to the Moon. "Lunatic" is the derivation of the Latin word *luna*, meaning the Moon. There are many colloquialisms which refer to our impressions of the Moon's influence such as *lunatic, lunacy, loony, moony, mooning, moonshadow, moonstruck, moon child, moonlighting, moonshine, moon blind*, and *moon calf*.

The Moon is said to have the power to change a person into a werewolf. Not many people believe that complete changes in personality or physical attributes occur because of the full Moon; however, there is still a belief the full Moon loosens inhibitions and increases our susceptibility to another's influence.

Throughout history, the time of the full Moon was said to transform otherwise sane people into lunatics. Insane asylum administrators of the eighteenth century were strong believers in the Moon's influence on the human psyche, so much so that they brought in additional staff members during the full Moon. The legal differences between just being affected by the Moon (a "lunatic") and actually being "insane" was set forth in law. One hundred years later, the Lunacy Act of 1842 referred to the changing of a person's mental state being linked with the changing phases of the Moon.

Today, staffs of hospital emergency rooms, ambulance services, and police and fire departments are aware of the changes occurring when the Moon is full. While being treated during a full Moon for a foot injury, my nurse related story after story of the emergency room becoming much busier during that time of the month. She jokingly said that some hospital workers schedule their days off during the full Moon in order to miss the rush.

I discussed the effects of the full Moon with the chief of security for a large, local, department store chain. He told me that shoplifting increased dramatically during the full Moon and they scheduled extra security personnel to deal with this increase.

Psychiatrists have conducted many experiments to further understand the Moon's effects on humanity. Records indicate a substantial rise in admittance to mental hospitals during the full Moon. The frequency of rapes, assaults, arson, homicides, suicides, and other violent crimes increase around the time of the new and full Moons. There have also been many studies attempting to determine the extent of the Moon's effect on the human mind and on the ability to commit criminal acts, as seen in a number of studies discussed in *Supernature.*

One such study in Ohio found admittance to psychiatric hospitals due to emotional breakdown significantly increased on and around full Moons. In another study the statistical evidence of criminal activity in Florida between the years of 1956 of 1970 was examined. The study found evidence of an increase in murders at the time of the new and full Moons. A similar set of circumstances was found to exist during the same time frame (1956 to 1970) in Dade County, Florida, where 1,887 murders were analyzed. Further studies conducted in Ohio found that the criminal activity did in fact peak, not at the new and full Moons, but three days afterwards. This delay was explained by the fact that Ohio sits in more northerly latitudes.

Scientist Andrija Puharich studied the possibility of increased psychic awareness and telepathic abilities during the new and full Moons. His results led him to conclude gravitational forces causing the tides are also at work on human consciousness. In *Beyond Telepathy*, Puharich details his test procedures and results. He prepared for five years to complete one lunar month of testing. Testing was accomplished through the use of matched sets of cards and a controlled environment. Results indicated a pronounced increase in telepathic abilities at the full Moon and a slightly less significant increase at the new Moon.

Further corroboration comes from a neurologist named Dr. Leonard Ravity, as discussed in *Witchcraft for Tomorrow* by Doreen Valiente. Dr. Ravity studied the flow of the electrical impulses in the brain, concluding that the Moon has an increased effect of lunacy on people already considered unstable. Measuring the microamperes flowing along the neural paths of the brain, Dr. Ravity found these currents increased dramatically during the new Moon and even more so during the full Moon.

The emotional responses each of us have to the Moon's changing phases and astrological signs may not be as obvious as those studied at psychiatric hospitals, but they are real. Happiness, sadness, vigor, lethargy, irritability, and emotional instability are all enhanced by the Moon. Our understanding of these lunar cycles allows us to use the Moon's power constructively.

Chapter 2

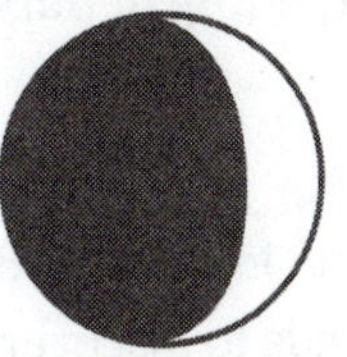

Using the Moon

Subtle emotional changes occur as the Moon travels through the heavens. These changes follow a cycle in conjunction with the Moon's cycle. Accurately forecasting these cyclical influences facilitates better control of our lives and dramatically increases our happiness. When we know the coming weekend will be a great time to socialize, it makes sense to be with friends, rather than with a book. Recognition of these emotional cycles is the key.

Recognition breeds predictability and comes with self-awareness. Self-awareness only comes from practice. It's surprising to discover how little we actually know about ourselves, and even more surprising to find how much less we're willing to admit. Self-awareness is increased through very simple exercises, such as journal writing. Achieving a better understanding of ourselves promotes compassion toward others.

The Journal

The journal is the basis of self-discovery. Writing about feelings leads to discovering hidden truths. A journal provides a means of privately exploring emotional reactions while comparing them to previous situations. This journal has nothing to do with the physical world—it's a place to honestly record feelings. A journal is not to replace intimate conversations with friends; rather, it's a safe place to honestly communicate with yourself.

Write in it after a salt bath or meditation, or when feeling the need to talk. (A salt bath is a form of emotional cleansing and meditation. Draw a warm bath and in it dissolve two or three tablespoons of sea salt. Place some candles around the edge of the tub, turn off the light and close the door. Relax and let the troubles of the day be drawn from your body into the water. Let your mind go.)

Dreams are another good topic for a journal. They often portray a simple message even though the circumstances may be bizarre. One theory of dream interpretation holds that the many characters in a dream represent different aspects of the dreamer.

The only information essential to each journal entry is the date, time, and the Sun and Moon signs. To determine the Sun and Moon signs, you will need an astrological calendar or ephemeris.

Do not use a tape recorder. Write by hand or type on a computer. The act of writing slows the thought processes and enhances attention to detail. Writing helps to cut out wishful thinking and the lies we tell ourselves, and to focus on our true emotions.

My journal writing consists of one or two-page stories about anything that catches my eye. I have found my emotional state is clearly expressed in my tales. Once I wrote about a lonely beer bottle sitting on the table next to me rather than in the recycling bin with all its friends.

Avoid meditation when the Moon is void of course. During this period of time the lunar influences are not clearly understood. The Moon is beginning to take on the characteristics of the coming astrological sign but has not completely abandoned the last sign. Many people "feel" the next Moon sign's effect strongest near the moment when the void of course Moon enters the next sign. For these people, the void of course Moon's effect will be typical, but not absolute. It is symbolized on the astrological calendar by a crescent Moon followed by "v/c" and a time. The Moon goes void of course at the time indicated and returns when it moves into the next sign. See chapter 4 for a detailed discussion about the void of course Moon.

Lunar Emotions

Label one page of the journal for each Moon, for example, "Moon in Aries." This page is for general feelings about life, work, and relationships. Are you feeling organized, energized, intense, deeply thoughtful, anxious, sad, angry, happy, joyful, loving, secure, or insecure? Do you feel the need to laugh, talk, giggle, or just to have a good cry? Do you want to participate and share with others, or would you prefer to spend time alone? Do you feel like running away? Try to explain exactly how you feel about life in general. Remember, "I don't know how I feel," is a feeling, but it can also be an excuse for not recognizing or admitting the truth. Every time the Aries Moon comes around, turn back to the Aries Moon sheet and review the entries for possible additions.

The Energy Log

Another self-discovery technique that I recommend is the energy log. Updated regularly, the energy log tracks the level of physical energy we experience. Everyone's energy fluctuates. On some days we feel supercharged and on others we drag. We enjoy wonderful, restful sleep on some nights, but only sleep fitfully on other nights. By tracking energy levels over a period of time, the Moon's effect on daily activities becomes apparent.

Fill out one of these forms every day. The upper portion includes the day and date as well as the sign and phase of the Moon. For women, it is important to track the menstrual cycle, which often occurs in conjunction with the lunar cycle, and can add energy to emotions.

Begin each morning by filling in the form. Make note of your energy level upon waking. Don't worry about the exact time, use the closest hour. Placing an "X" or a dot in the square representing the time and the level of energy is sufficient. Record your energy level each hour for the rest of the day. Again, this doesn't have to be done exactly on the hour. Recording it every three or four hours will be fine. There is no need to awaken during the night to fill in the form; however, evaluating the night's sleep the following morning is important.

This technique provides an understanding of daily energy-level fluctuations and teaches the ability to instantly recognize when they occur and why. A poor night's rest will no longer be a mystery. A great day will no longer be an accident.

Here is an example to be used as a basis for the zero to ten energy scale:

0 dead to the world

1 an alcohol or drug-induced sleep

2 a deep sleep

3 a normal, restful sleep

4 a light sleep

5 starting to move—needing that first cup of coffee

6 a low energy day—the blahs

7 an average day

8 an up day—feeling pretty good

9 an exciting and energized day

10 an intensely excited state—walking on fire

Any scale will be satisfactory. The goal is to learn what level of intensity or energy may be expected from each Moon. The link between personal energy levels and the Moon's cycle will become obvious, as will the body's unique energy signature. Everyone's energy fluctuates throughout the day in fairly predictable patterns.

On the back, bottom, or other empty space on the energy log, briefly describe the day's activities and your personal level of participation. Were you fully present at all times, or were you distracted, and why?

Once you have kept the journal for a month the information collected needs to be analyzed. Search for repetition in the charts and journal information. Look for repeated feelings, emotions, and energy levels. The research may indicate that a Virgo Moon is best used for analytical tasks and is the perfect Moon to summarize the results.

The Moon is a positive influence as it passes through our natal Sun signs, and brings extra energy and feelings of joy. Almost anything can be accomplished without dreading the work. This is true with every person to varying degrees. Conversely, when the Moon is in the Sun's opposite sign, it will produce challenging times and decrease energy levels. This is also a phenomenon common to everyone, but in differing intensities.

The following is a list of the Sun signs arranged in opposites. Look for your Sun sign and next to it will be the opposite sign. With this information you can glance at the upper right hand corner of your astrological calendar and quickly determine which days will be the most joyful and rewarding days, and which days will be the most difficult and challenging:

- Aries/Libra
- Taurus/Scorpio
- Gemini/Sagittarius
- Cancer/Capricorn
- Leo/Aquarius
- Virgo/Pisces

Energy Log

Date:__/__/__ Day:__________

Moon Phase:__________ Moon Sign:__________

Day of Menstruation:__________ Average Energy Level:__________

Work Hours:__________ Sleep Hours:__________

Time	0	1	2	3	4	5	6	7	8	9	10
12 A.M.											
1 A.M.											
2 A.M.											
3 A.M.											
4 A.M.											
5 A.M.											
6 A.M.											
7 A.M.											
8 A.M.											
9 A.M.											
10 A.M.											
11 A.M.											
12 P.M.											
1 P.M.											
2 P.M.											
3 P.M.											
4 P.M.											
5 P.M.											
6 P.M.											
7 P.M.											
8 P.M.											
9 P.M.											
10 P.M.											
11 P.M.											

When the Moon is in Taurus, my Sun sign, I am energized, full of life, and have an overwhelming desire to play. Conversely, when the Moon is Scorpio, my energy level is low.

Examine the completed energy chart for days with increased or decreased energy. Look for patterns and cycles. Start your investigation by examining the morning hours. Do you move slowly after awakening in the morning? Does it take you a long time to get moving, and then only after two cups of coffee? If normally slow starting, look for days with increased energy levels earlier in your day. Was there a day, or series of days, when you jumped out of bed? Did you experience one or more days with an extra bounce in your step or in which you sang all the way to work?

Next, focus on the late morning and afternoon, and then the evening and night. How did you sleep? Were you up and down all night? Did you close your eyes and open them to find morning had arrived? Did you dream? Were your dreams so intense they actually interrupted your sleep?

These patterns provide a glimpse of the Moon's influence. A series of days in a particular mood is the easiest indicator to recognize. A single passionate day is not necessarily important. Recognizing a series of days will quickly become easy. This proficiency will extend to single days or even moments of lunar influence.

I have discovered many things through this analysis. My best times to write are mornings and late evenings. At midday, my mind is so occupied with other things that I can't stay focused long enough to be productive in my writing. I have found that the Virgo Moon is particularly conducive to editing and the Gemini Moon enhances creativity.

A monthly lunar summary (see page 22) can help you to find cyclical emotional patterns. Plot the average energy level from the daily energy charts in a month against the days the Moon spent in each Zodiac sign. This will give you a better feel for the differences of the signs.

Look for patterns. A one-month period may begin to show a cycle in your emotional responses and behavior. Extending this charting over a longer period will increase the accuracy of your analysis.

Use this chart to examine particular times of the day. If six o'clock in the evening is often challenging, use this exercise to closely examine your emotional susceptibility to lunar influences at that time. You need only chart your energy level at six o'clock every day and look for a pattern to emerge.

Make a mental note whenever you feel emotionally attached to a particular situation or experience. Check the Moon sign in comparison to your emotions. A pattern may emerge indicating a tendency to respond generically during that particular Moon sign. I am quick to lose my temper in an Aries Moon. I will banter with others in an Aquarius Moon, but am less willing to share my personal life.

The Cancer Moon has been my best teacher of self-honesty and responsibility. I used to lie to myself about my life and my relationships, and blamed everyone else for my problems. My mood would change quickly when I was faced with the truth. I couldn't hold back the tears. Once the Cancer Moon had cracked my emotional dam, I was flooded by the resulting torrential flow of emotion. Over time, these waters receded and were replaced with self-honesty. I discovered that the only person who believed my lies was me and I accepted responsibility for my experiences.

Monthly Lunar Summary

Month:___________

Day	Moon Sign	0	1	2	3	4	5	6	7	8	9	10

When I hear myself placing blame on another, I immediately "check in" to see who is responsible. By subsequently dropping the whole notion in favor of accepting responsibility, I sidestep the emotional blocks of blame and victimhood.

This is your life, not the Zodiac's. Everything that you do and say, and all of your responses to the stimuli in your life, are your responsibility. I am a believer in the rule of three: my actions return to me three times. Therefore, I take responsibility for the things that happen in my life.

Chapter 3

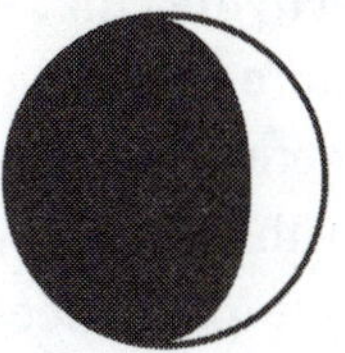

The Moon's Phases

Each phase of the Moon can exert its influence upon any situation. We know that the new and full Moons increase our emotional sensitivity. The waxing and waning Moons can also be influential.

The first quarter, or new Moon, is a time for new beginnings. The solar and lunar energies come together and pull in the same direction, which provides a thrust of new life. Beginnings come to pass as instinctive or intuitive actions. Since all is hidden from light at the dark Moon, dreams and waking inspirations often hold the answers. Our inner-self naturally listens to the rhythms of the world and is aware of the unseen.

Shortly before the new Moon, a New Age bookstore owner told me her story. Apparently, she was so busy with her daily activities that she seldom found time to read the books in her store. Around the time of the new Moon, her intuitive abilities were at their strongest, and she was able to recommend books without reading them. She matched her "feelings" about a person to her "feelings" about a book. The feedback she received from her customers was very positive.

Toward the end of the first quarter, the Moon and Sun are no longer in relative alignment. The Moon exerts a stronger influence; it maintains its energetic presence but is no longer added to by the Sun. The Moon's and Sun's energies will be combined again at the full Moon, when they are opposed to each other. Until then, the newly-formed crescent Moon shines and grows, nurturing all that is positive. This is the time to finalize plans and make progress. Gather your energies and direct them toward new goals.

The second quarter is a time to work on things already started. Apply active energy towards completing, producing, or adding to previously initiated projects or activities. Under the steadily growing light of the Moon, progress toward goals should be well under way. As the full Moon approaches, the final touches should be put in place to perfect that which is desired.

Michael manufactures magical knives (*athames* and *bolines*) by hand for a select clientele. He is very particular, as are his customers, about the phase of the Moon when he's crafting these knives. He will only forge, temper, and hone blades or fashion the handles during the Moon's first and second quarters. He polishes the blades, decorates the handles, and sews the sheaths in the last few days of the second quarter, and completes his knives by the full Moon.

The third quarter begins with the full Moon, which signals the time for completion. What was begun at the new Moon has progressed to maturity. The full Moon represents the peak of lunar, life-giving energies and, when coupled with the opposing solar energies, we receive all that nature has to offer. This is the time when effort meets its purpose. Our work is complete, and we should put to use what we worked so hard to create. Fulfillment is the primary directive as we near the last quarter. The original thought has become reality. As this quarter progresses, begin to consider the excess that needs to be reduced.

The fourth quarter is a time for destruction or disintegration. It is a time to eliminate the unnecessary in order to make room for the new. We have celebrated our success long enough. Now we must rid ourselves of old thoughts and plans to make room for new inspirations. This is the time to dismantle that which has been productive in order to eventually make room for new life in the freshly fertilized ground. The light is decreasing as darkness begins to take control. Michael cuts his stock and cleans his forge during the Moon's last quarter.

When the need for destruction arises, it should be brought to light during the third quarter and allowed to die, as with all things during the last two quarters of the Moon. The dark Moon arrives with lessons of its own. The Moon is dark in the last days of this quarter, which is nature's time to rest and recuperate. Upon completing the cycle of birth, life, and death, the soul remains in this darkness to concentrate on the lessons of this incarnation. These teachings remain in the forefront of thought, and must be condensed and converted to a vision to be built upon in the next life. It is in this phase that the past makes a commitment to the future. Introspection is a key word for the dark Moon. Since most of the work that occurs during the dark

Moon is of an intuitive nature, intentions and affirmations are the best hope for permanently laying to rest that which is dead.

The shift from light to darkness and back again is a natural phenomenon. As the Moon revolves around the earth and the earth revolves around the Sun, there is always a dark and a light side. Darkness has often been associated with evil, and light is usually considered to hold the goodness of all things. This belief probably came about because darkness hides all within its realm, while light is seemingly transparent and open by nature. These beliefs are somewhat unfortunate because each of us has a dark side—a hidden inner-self. Meditation gives us access to our darkness and raises our level of consciousness so that we might understand the relationship between the dark and light aspects that comprise the soul.

In astrology, the temple of the soul is symbolized by the Moon. The earliest religious teachers, and teachers of today, insist all things must be in balance. The soul is no exception, and must be balanced between the dark and light aspects. Each of these aspects carries its own stream of life: light, associated with the Sun; and darkness, associated with the Moon. The Sun, and the life energy we receive from it, is related to the productive, outer persona. This is the part of our being which deals with the daily activities and controls our waking hours. The Sun provides life and energy. It vitalizes all parts of our physical body.

Studies have been shown that depression sets in when the human body does not get enough exposure to the Sun. This type of depression is known as seasonal affective disorder. According to Dr. Robert M. Giller and Kathy Matthews in their book *Natural Prescriptions,* seasonal affective disorder is a form of depression that is apparently related to retinal stimulation by light. Seasonal affective disorder is four times more prevalent in women and is suffered by 5 percent of the northern populations. Differing from other forms of depression, it primarily affects people during the winter months. Those affected by seasonal affective disorder complain of loss of energy, increased anxiety, decreased sexual interest, oversleeping, overeating, and weight gain.

I was born in the Desert Southwest. At the age of thirty-seven I moved to Portland, Oregon, where the weather is the exact opposite of my birthplace. In the Pacific Northwest misty, overcast days are commonplace—so common, in fact, that inhabitants celebrate sunny days. Even during the winter months, Portlanders don shorts and t-shirts when the Sun shows its shining face. They appreciate the Sun—they relish the days when it shines. When the Sun hasn't been out for an extended period of time, people become restless, irritable, and depressed.

The "dark side" of our being is represented by the Moon. This is our invisible side, which is normally active during the night, when the conscious mind is at rest. The lunar-self is composed of the superconscious and subconscious minds. In numerology, the Moon is associated with the number two; it represents both sides of life, the light and the dark, and the duality of the soul.

Our soul is this energy. It feeds all that we are and all that we'll become. Deep within the recesses of the soul lie our secrets, memories, fears, and past lives in their entirety. Imagine the soul as the ocean. It is boundless. Within it we find history and the many lives that have come before. Just as the ocean is all encompassing, so are the soul and the subconscious mind through the collective unconscious.

Psychologist Carl Jung developed the theory of the collective unconscious to explain the "connections" we have to each other and our past lives. He conducted experiments that showed an astrological compatibility between married couples that far exceeded mere chance. He theorized that we are collectively connected by a consciousness that is otherwise undetectable. It can be explored with the requisite amount of courage and honesty.

We are often reminded of our past lives. A typical example is when we meet someone and feel as though we have known them all our lives. The subconscious mind taps into the collective unconscious and recalls our joint history. Rather than remembering that history, we feel an instant connection to our "old friend," by recognizing some quality of their personality we have always enjoyed.

The inner world is the place to which we withdraw for revitalization. This occurs every night during sleep. Our dreams work out problems on a deeper level than we often allow ourselves to consciously see. This re-energizing of the soul also occurs at death, when we examine what was accomplished in the last life and make plans for the next one.

As the ocean is the source of all life, the soul's energy is the source of our inner strength, without which the outer-self could not function. The masculine personality can only be fed from the feminine inner-self. We are the product of our soul, which has been shaped and molded through many lifetimes, and of our ego, which masks our true personality from the world at large. This protective mechanism is an essential part of our being, but at times does get in the way of integrity. By allowing honesty to flourish within, we can bring the ego into balance, thus demonstrating to ourselves and the world the real, wonderful person behind the mask.

Chapter 4

Moon Sign Effects

The Moon's never-ending journey through the heavens brings to us a source of energy and influence. In some ways, the Moon's influence is constant, dependable, and predictable; in other ways, it is always changing. Each full Moon is associated with a particular astrological sign and occurs in the same solar month every year, and the same is true for new Moons. The Taurus full Moon shines every year when the Sun is in Scorpio, which opposes Taurus, and the Taurus new Moon occurs when the Sun is in Taurus. This consistent pattern is set against the variability of when the full and new Moons occur during any given month, and the Moon's changing phases.

The energetic influence of the Moon on our bodies, minds, and souls exhibits the same constantly changing dichotomy as its physical presence in our lives. Consistency comes from the Moon's cyclical motion, which constantly exerts its primeval tug. The differences lie in the astrological signs and the Moon's phases. As the Moon moves from sign to sign, and from phase to phase, its influence on us changes in both substance and intensity.

Added to these changes are the many different combinations of Moon signs and Moon phases that we experience during the Moon's Metonic cycle. The Moon's Metonic cycle refers to the Moon's nineteen-year cycle, which was discovered by an Athenian astronomer, Meton. Approximately every nineteen years, the new Moon occurs on the same day. This alone makes the Moon both mathematically predictable and curiously unpredictable.

In the following pages, we will explore each Moon sign's influence upon us. This information is included as a basis for discovering and differentiating between the Moon's effect on our emotions from each particular astrological sign. The statements are generalized and may not apply to everyone, since there are other factors at work, such as the Moon's phase and the other planets in the natal horoscope. Use the information presented as a reference. Relating this information to our experiences helps us to understand ourselves and serves as a basis for understanding the changes we undergo as the Moon travels along its celestial highway.

Lunar Influences of the Aries Moon

As the Moon passes through Aries, everyone, regardless of their Moon or Sun sign, will receive a good dose of Aries energy. This can be very positive or negative depending on our ability to absorb and deal with this influx of energy. The Aries Moon will add fuel to whatever fire might be burning at the time. A calm, or even sedate, relationship could flare up with excitement, or a situation on the verge of losing control will explode with intensity, depending on the underlying influences.

Don't plan on sleeping late or just lying around in front of the television during an Aries Moon. This is a time for getting things done. Use its energy to benefit by starting something that has been put off for a while. Stay focused on things that need extra attention. If life should be intense while the Moon is in Aries, understand that the energy received greatly intensifies emotions. Our feelings are more easily hurt and we will be quick to respond with verbal attacks.

Nancy, a dear friend, and I become short-tempered during the Aries Moon. We have learned that when an Aries Moon comes around, we must avoid each other or be unusually aware of our words and deeds. This is especially true over the phone because body language is not available to tell the unspoken story. A smile following a sentence can make a tremendous difference.

The Aries Moon should be used to accomplish things from which you will get some satisfaction upon completion. This Moon will certainly push us forward if some degree of pride or recognition will be the reward. A challenging but fun activity or project is best.

Lunar Influences of the Taurus Moon

The Moon in Taurus personality is one of comfort, dependability, steadfastness, and stability. Taurus is a Feminine, Earth sign.

Our level of patience will increase. We may respond to people in a subdued manner, at least until we've reached our emotional limit. Once there, tempers could flare like supernovas, allowing basic instincts to take control. The Taurus Moon enhances willpower; this Moon will help in the completion of previously started tasks, but will hinder starting something new.

Depending on the phase of the Moon and other circumstances, the Taurus Moon's lunar influences may be perceived as negative. Personal energy levels may seem reduced. The Taurus Moon is the first Earth sign and promotes grounding, with deep roots like an old-growth tree. We may be inclined to hold back and not get involved; it would be so much easier to take a nap. However, when in a space to receive the positive influences of this Moon, our energy level increases dramatically.

I'm very comfortable with Taurus Moon energies and become invigorated by them. The Taurus Moon is probably the most joyful and productive time for me. There are other Moons in which I experience joy and pleasure, but there are few Moons which are as consistently productive.

Big changes aren't in the stars during this Moon. Stability is a buzzword for the those affected by a Taurus Moon. Venturing off the beaten path is not easily accomplished unless you are very motivated; however, this stability will breed greater inner strength from which inner joy will grow.

This Moon will not be an easy time to share possessions. Taurean Moon and Sun signs are fairly materialistic and, under the

Taurus Moon's influence, we feel the same way. Along the same lines, if we borrow other people's possessions, it requires taking very good care of them.

This is a good time to deal with financial matters. Your practical nature will be intensified and money matters will be a little less mystifying. Learn to save money in all Earth Moons, especially this one, as your need for preservation of resources will be greater.

The materialism of this Moon will entice you to buy things that you desire but would otherwise forego. I have experienced this feeling many times and have found it difficult to override. A good compromise for me is to go shopping for groceries.

You will feel much more secure in this Moon. In addition to promoting security and patience, the Taurus Moon will enhance stubbornness and drive. Upon finding the exact item for which you've been searching, you will purchase it without a second thought. This will be especially true if the object of desire is one of beauty, love, or stature.

The inner strength and stubbornness of the Bull, along with its practical nature, will help you to attain any goal, assuming the process has already started. The Taurus Moon will generally allow two choices: to sit and wait to see what happens, or to complete something previously begun. New endeavors are not usually an option.

This Moon will bring out your supportive and caring nature. You might even be described as sensitive. The connection between this Moon and its opposite sign, Scorpio, as well as the connection between the Moon and Cancer will bring out the romantic in you. Initiating a new relationship in this Moon would not be my first choice, but pursuing an existing one works well.

Lunar Influences of the Gemini Moon

Represented in the heavens by the Twins, the influence of the Gemini Moon on your personality will make you feel as though you are twins, but not identical twins. You will be easily split between the outer solar-self and inner lunar-self. During this Moon the inner-self may remain hidden deep inside the darkness, while the outer persona denies its existence. This dichotomy can cause an internal conflict, which, if not managed carefully, will cause frequent mood swings.

The Gemini Moon will enhance your extroverted qualities, which could be put to good use in dealing with others. The mind will move from one thing to another very quickly, almost instantaneously. If the "gift of gab" is something you've always wanted, you will find it in this Moon. Alert and creative, your ability to carry on a conversation with others will be improved by a quick and sharp sense of humor. This could get out of hand if the conversation becomes flirtatious.

Instinctual responses will be at their height; your first reaction will probably be the best reaction. The Gemini Moon is a time for enjoying people and having fun. Communication skills will be at their peak, and your energy level will be enough for two. Avoid becoming impatient with others—it is a real possibility in your energized state. The Gemini Moon is restless. You will flit from one thought to another, and from one conversation to another, not so much from a lack of direction as from mere restlessness. This is an Air Moon, so flightiness is to be expected.

The quickening of the intellect that occurs during this Moon may be used to solve problems that have weighed you down, especially during the Taurus Moon. Love relationships fall under this rational influence, which can yield positive solutions to difficult emotional problems. While intuition is of great use, your willingness to listen in this Moon is very low.

I find this Moon's influence to be confusing. On one hand, I want to be open and communicative, while on the other, I want to hide. The polarity of this Moon is difficult for me to fully integrate, and makes it less comfortable for me than other Moons.

Lunar Influences of the Cancer Moon

Buckle your seat belt because this Moon can be quite a ride. Cancer is ruled by the Moon, and the Cancer Moon's influence is deep and intense. Cancer is a Feminine, Water sign and, with its lunar ruler, will intensify the full range of emotions—from the highest of highs to the lowest of lows. The Moon's phases in Cancer also greatly affect your emotional state.

The Cancer Moon will allow you to understand the inner-self by exploring your emotions. It is time for those feelings, suppressed for so long, to come to the surface and be noticed. If the Moon feeds your soul, this Moon is like an intravenous line to the heart.

In this Moon I'm subject to quick emotional reactions. Intense, emotional situations, including those portrayed in movies and books, strike me deeply. I can't tell you how many times I have cried at a cheesy heroic scene in a less than award-winning movie, or was sent deep into introspection after becoming engrossed in a truly beautiful movie experience.

This is not a Moon that can be readily "used" for your own agenda; it will use you. The only way to deal with this Moon in a positive manner is to be honest with yourself, not just during this Moon but at all times. It is dishonesty that traps emotional monsters in the depths of your inner-self. The Cancer Moon has an uncanny way of releasing these monsters. There is no way to stop or to hide from a Cancer Moon.

The best course of action to minimize the effects of a Cancer Moon is to open yourself to it. Be prepared to listen to what your inner voice has to say. The willingness to be a good listener is essential because it will get the point across, one way or another.

Listen to and learn from your soul. Your inner-self is trying to show you the things that you lock up inside and refuse to recognize. You may see the difference between who you really are and the image you project to the world. As you become more open and honest with yourself, you will begin to show the world your true self. As this happens, the inner and outer-selves begin to come together, and reflect the same personal characteristics. In doing so, you will lessen the likelihood that repressed emotions will be trapped in the darkness of the psyche, waiting to attack. You may also find that the world at large likes the person you really are, much more so than the person you want them to see.

I have found that I am more honest with myself in this Moon than in others. In the Cancer Moon I trust my feelings and emotions, and am undaunted by ego-based lies.

Several years ago, I had difficulty living with personal integrity as I went through a divorce. It was hard to determine exactly how I felt about myself and others, or about my job and my life as a whole, because the lies I told myself were designed to protect my ego. At this point I became a jumble of emotions and completely useless during the Cancer Moon. I could do nothing but cry. Once I recognized that these few days of each month should be a time of honest self-analysis, I was able to take advantage of this insight and began to put my life in order. The honest self-analysis achieved in the Cancer Moon allowed me to determine what I wanted out of life. I then attained my desires by setting goals and charting a course towards achieving them. Although the Cancer Moon can be the most troublesome Moon, it can also be the most rewarding.

Lunar Influences of the Leo Moon

As the Moon passes into Leo, you may experience a warm feeling of relief. This Fire sign exudes pride, warmth, and generosity, along with dominance, extravagance, and righteousness. When affected by this sign, you could become quite dramatic in your actions and demand admiration from others.

The Lion is King of the Jungle. When the Moon is in Leo you want to rule over your domain. Ruled by the Sun, the Leo Moon is Masculine and will help you to reveal your feelings to others. Your flamboyant charm attracts attention, and your warm, dignified demeanor captures the appreciation of others. Be careful not to be too stubborn or opinionated. Pride and the domination of others can undermine or negate the acceptance and appreciation you seek.

This can be a time to just bask in the Sun on the beach. The Leo Moon has a fiery sort of energy, but its influence is more in the realm of personality than in action. Tell a good story and give plenty of advice, but don't do anything more strenuous than applying tanning lotion.

I have done exactly that in Leo Moons—lie on the beach. I usually feel as though I have just finished a workout—warm and recovering, with things to do but preferring to rest.

Don't plan to use Leo's energy for anything constructive. It's best used to recuperate from the difficult emotional workout you had in the last Moon, and to show off your progress at becoming emotionally fit. Relax and enjoy life without the pressures of inner or outer strife.

Your intuition will work well in the realm of social interactions rather than emotions. Use your charm to connect with people because you will intuitively know what they need. You will be generous and affectionate as long as you have the spotlight. Lean toward the dignified and the proud when searching for glory among those you have charmed.

Lunar Influences of the Virgo Moon

When the Moon passes into Virgo it will provide solid, earthy stability and an affinity for detailed analysis. You will not be as lethargic as in the Taurus Moon, but Virgo can put a damper on things. The tendency towards detailed analysis doesn't only apply to situations and people, but to your own emotions and emotional behavior. This may manifest to the extent that all you have time for is worry. The Virgo Moon will also add a critical side to your personality. If you're already a critical person, friends and associates had better beware. This Moon will help you to criticize anything and everything. The analytical characteristics of the Virgo Moon could cause distrust of others. It may also lead to withdrawal.

I ask a lot of questions in this Moon, sometimes feeling like my eight-year-old son, who asks "why" in every sentence. Although part of his questioning is due to his age, the Virgo Moon intensifies this trait in him as well.

Not all of Virgo's lunar influences are negative. Actually, very positive changes can occur during the Virgo Moon. You may feel an urge to work hard and complete a project that you've been putting off for some time. This Moon will improve intuitive powers. Thanks to your insightful and clear-headed intuition, you will be able to discern the truth of a situation without knowing all of the facts. The details and trivialities of life may need some attention and, with the Moon's help, you will have the patience to give them their due.

The Virgo Moon will send a burst of focused intensity that you can use to feel quietly immovable. There are many ways that the Virgo Moon's energy can be used to benefit life: delve into financial planning, such as evaluating mutual funds; critique the performance of politicians running for office before an election; or, use your enhanced intuition and the slightly romantic energies of this Moon to improve a love relationship. Just use your intuition.

Lunar Influences of the Libra Moon

The sign of Libra is represented by the Scales, and the influence of the Moon in Libra is to keep the emotional scales balanced. This is an Air sign, so there will be moments of indecision—perhaps more aptly described as moments of decisiveness in a sea of indecision. During this Moon you may have difficulty in deciding how you feel, even though at some level you know.

I become terribly indecisive and unfocused during the few days of the Libra Moon. The easiest choices are the most difficult—whether to eat at home or go out to dinner, which movie to rent, which CD to play, or how to dress. I'm terribly susceptible to distractions. I have walked out of my apartment without my keys and have locked my keys in my truck. I have forgotten where I am going, and how to address an envelope after sealing the letter inside.

Just as you feel that your emotions should be in balance, you also want others to create a well-balanced environment. Inharmonious behavior will upset your sense of fairness, and force you to express your feelings (with tact, of course, because your charm is still working).

You will feel a renewed closeness to your loved ones. The Libra Moon exaggerates the need for companionship in both love and business. This can occur to the point of insecurity. It might be important to wait a few days before making any decisions involving a new partnership or the future of a relationship until the insecurity of this Moon passes. One thing is for certain—you will expect to be treated the same way that you treat others.

It is difficult at best to have faith in yourself in this Moon. The tools are at hand to hear the words from within, but you will probably be unwilling to act on them. Emotional insecurity is a byproduct of this Moon, along with feelings of inadequacy. Relief from these feelings must come from within. Unfortunately, it is easier to seek relief in a love relationship.

Overall, this Moon is a good one for the love life. You will feel a romantic tug at your heart and an appreciation for the beauty in all things. Your charm and diplomacy will make it easier to deal with people. The inability to make a decision will pass. In the meantime, try to not put yourself in a situation where decisions must be made.

You may become so indecisive in a Libra Moon that life becomes humorous. Unfortunately, your indecisiveness can exasperate the people around you.

Lunar Influences of the Scorpio Moon

"Intensity" is the best word to describe the influence that this Moon will bring. Intensity in all things will be emphasized, but especially in your relationships with others. As the Moon enters Scorpio, psychic and intuitive abilities are greatly improved. It will be easier for you to "know" how others are feeling.

The Scorpio Moon is a Water Moon, so your emotional responses will be enhanced and emotional needs will be magnified. It would be wise to hold back from intense emotional encounters, especially those that might be negative. It will take very little provocation to cause a rage, because emotions are already elevated.

Good emotional sense will be reduced and you may become quite uninhibited. This lack of inhibitions may make it more likely that you will prematurely intensify a relationship.

Sexual desire is a major effect of the Scorpio Moon. Your personality will become more irresistible, and you will feel very sensual. The knowledge that you have an increased sex drive for a few days should help you to moderate the decisions you make in relationships.

Mental processes will also be enhanced during this Moon due to heightened intuitive powers. You will be more insightful when it comes to research and problem solving. This is not an analytical Moon sign, unlike the Virgo Moon, but you will "just know" the answer or, at a minimum, know where to look.

Mental self-discipline will be at an all-time high—you will feel unbeatable. With this commitment and confidence you are able to pursue and accomplish any goal, but it must be something that you desire because it is emotional interest that drives you.

Secrecy could be a problem during this Moon. You may be unwilling to divulge any information about yourself unless, of course, it involves sex, or something as intensely emotional and passionate. On the other hand, you will ask very direct and pointed questions about any subject, including sex, to just about anyone, especially your closest friends. Even when talking about sex, you will hold back. The Scorpio Moon cannot give up all of her secrets.

Lunar Influences of the Sagittarius Moon

The Sagittarius Moon is a Fire Moon. Under this Moon the intensely sexual energies of the Scorpio Moon will turn to warm, romantic feelings. This is a great time for companionship, especially with someone who holds your romantic interest.

You will generally be optimistic and enthusiastic in this Moon. All of that Fire energy will help you to get going, but the forward momentum will be best used on projects that involve the spiritual realm, such as educational activities or religious studies.

The Sagittarius Moon is a controlling Moon. Control over life, regardless of the situation, is difficult. Avoid becoming upset if control evades your tactics. Although this isn't a Moon for fighting, you will be ruthless if needed.

Your optimism will be notched up by this Moon. Optimism is a good thing to have, but in this Moon excessive optimism will result in carelessness and the inability to see the truth until it is much too late.

I am usually relaxed and restless on the days of the Sagittarius Moon. My attitude toward work and the doldrums of normal life is relaxed—these things become less important, while my spiritual pursuits take top priority. Many of my passions take root in this Moon.

Spend some time with your favorite charity or organization, though you may not feel like participating in group activities. Anything that focuses your energy for the greater good will be beneficial. You will become very restless in this Moon; try to stay focused at work or through your own passionate pursuits. At home don't expect your companion to follow your lead; restlessness and a possible lack of focus could lead to trouble.

The Sagittarius Moon is a time to be idealistic and work toward your highest goals, especially those with an emotional appeal. Travel is also a draw right now, but be careful—this extra Fire energy may lead to a discussion about the speed limit with a law enforcement officer.

Lunar Influences of the Capricorn Moon

This is a Moon for getting things done. It is an Earth Moon, so you will feel grounded and practical. If you are motivated by personal goals and achievements, this is a sign that will spur your ambition. This is also a Moon in which you may want to withdraw emotionally.

There may be a tradeoff in your approach to life during this Moon. You may lean towards materialistic concerns, but your intuition will be at work, though emotionally suppressed by the Capricorn Moon's grounding qualities. Stuffing your emotions deep down inside is a danger during this Moon. You may feel detached, and others may feel that you are aloof.

Clean out a closet or the garage. You'll have the workhorse energy to get any job done and a less-than-sentimental detachment that allows you to throw things away that you might otherwise talk yourself into keeping. This could also be a good time to work on budgets and bills.

I always seem to balance my checkbook in a Capricorn Moon. I often procrastinate where my checkbook is concerned, but the Capricorn Moon gives me the motivation necessary to get the work done. This Moon grounds me sufficiently so I can accept bad news, such as forgetting to write down ATM withdrawals.

On the other hand, this is not a good time on work on spiritual matters or matters of the heart. There's an inclination towards separation from your feelings that makes it unwise to deal with others and their feelings. You'll leave others with the impression that you're cold and heartless. The interesting part of this scenario is you're certainly not cold and heartless, but, in this Moon, your emotions run very still and very deep. So deep, in fact, that you won't look at them.

Take this opportunity to focus on work and complete some of those things that have been nagging you. Know that you may not be prepared to deal with emotional issues, so they may be best left alone.

Lunar Influences of the Aquarius Moon

You will be everybody's friend in this Moon. With this Moon's outgoing and imaginative energies, you're equipped to help others with humanitarian pursuits.

Idealistic lunar pressure will influence you right now, as if it was left over from the last Moon; however, instead of withdrawing, there will be a willingness to discuss your thoughts with anyone who will listen. You may also be very blunt and say things that are meant to startle others. The shock value of your statements will be weighed prior to speaking them—the more shocking the statement, the more fun you will have saying it.

Charisma will be in no short supply during this Moon. You can inspire others with enthusiasm and imagination. Your effect on others is solely due to the outer presentation of yourself, as your emotions will still be on the cool side.

Emotionally, you will desire privacy, because you feel distant from others and are unwilling to include them in your emotional life. This will contribute to the feeling that others have that they cannot get close to you or that you're hiding behind an outgoing, exciting persona.

This is a Moon that troubles me. I find difficulty in simultaneously desiring to be charismatic and private. I deal with others through intimacy and the need for privacy makes intimacy a real chore. Trying to deal with these two opposites confuses me, and I escape through detachment.

Freedom may top your list for the next few days, and fits in with the emotional detachment you're experiencing. The need for freedom will make you feel chained down when someone tries to get close. Take the initiative with friends and family—decide on things you want to do, and invite the others along. Your need for freedom will be satisfied and you will enjoy socializing with others.

Stay away from situations which require direction from others. Being told what to do will be difficult to accept in this Moon. Try to work on independent projects. The more control you have over your life the happier you will be.

Lunar Influences of the Pisces Moon

The last Moon in the Zodiac will influence you to be sensitive, compassionate, and psychic. In fact, the Pisces Moon will enhance your empathic and intuitive abilities more than any other Moon. The rub comes from your susceptibility to the opinions of others; you can be led to distrust your inner thoughts and feelings.

Your compassionate side will be in full swing during this Moon. You will be sensitive to everyone's feelings but your own, and will be inclined to help anyone in need. Don't take in too many stray dogs and cats. The danger is in giving too much of yourself and not saving your emotional energy for the person who needs the support the most—yourself. Helping those less fortunate is a noble task, but listen to you intuition; it knows when enough is enough.

My intuitive abilities increase dramatically in Water Moons, especially in the Pisces Moon. I work as a tarot reader for parties and individuals. I feel more comfortable reading the cards during a Pisces Moon because I find it easier to connect with my clients and Spirit.

I was out for a walk one evening during a Pisces Moon. The rain had just stopped and the air was warm. I was two blocks from my home when I saw a young lady pacing back and forth on the sidewalk, taking about six steps each direction. I asked her if she was all right. She looked and "felt" upset to me. Tears ran down her face as she looked at me and said she had just received happy news. I immediately responded, without knowing what my words meant. I told her the good news did not change anything, and that the guy still treated her horribly. The young lady looked at me in astonishment and asked in a whispering voice, "How did you know?"

Your imagination will be very active right now. If you're artistic, it's time to do some work. In fact, artistic expression is best-suited to the Pisces Moon, so conquer those projects that require creative thought.

The spiritual world could be a major focus during this Moon. This is not surprising as your empathic and psychic abilities are at their maximum. Religious endeavors are well advised and pursuing them will be inwardly rewarding. Any support you get will help to offset your emotional output to others.

In matters of love, be more careful than usual. During this Moon you are looking at things through the proverbial rose-colored glasses. Your feelings for another may be unusually strong due to your current emotional state. If you wear your heart on your sleeve under the empathic influence of this Moon, you could pick up on the feelings of others and mistake them for your own.

This is a wonderful Moon, but take care not to ignore the inner voice. Rely on your intuition; it really does know best. Taking heed of your inner voice will serve you well.

Void of Course Moon

When the Moon is about to move from one sign to another, there is a period in which the Moon will no longer be aspected to another planet while in that sign. The period of time between the last major aspect in that sign and the Moon entering the next sign is called "void of course." The major difficulty when the Moon is void of course is that it can cause our thoughts to be delusional. Therefore, the decisions made at these times will seldom, if ever, produce favorable results. Plans will fall apart and purchases will be faulty or will sit in the garage unused. Our perception becomes unrealistic and unreliable.

Luckily, the Moon does not stay void of course very long. Although our lives in this world must progress, stick with previously established plans while the Moon is void of course. Leave the decision making for another time. This is usually easy because the Moon will often be void of course in the middle of the night—not too many decisions need to be made while we're sleeping. It's not uncommon to feel unfocused, as though life has no direction. The best cure is to treat the void of course Moon as you would the dark Moon: turn inside and become better focused and centered.

An unusual astrological event occurred in the summer of 1996—the Moon was void of course for an unusually long time while most of the planets that could travel retrograde (in this case, Venus, Jupiter, Uranus, Neptune, and Pluto) were doing so. Retrograde motion as seen from the earth is the apparent reversal, or backward, motion of a planet through the cosmos. Mercury most often goes retrograde, and in doing so, appears to move backwards. When a planet is in retrograde, it affects our lives in an out of the ordinary manner. Mercury in retrograde degrades communication, especially in written forms. A large percentage of my friends, being wary of these astrological influences, decided to take this time off and do little or nothing. I had previously committed to attending a firewalk. On the evening of this notable astrological event I was walking on 1,200 °F coals and having a wonderful time.

Influence of the Moon's Phases

In an earlier chapter we discussed the Moon's phases and how they fit into the natural rhythms of life. Here we need to discuss how these same phases intensify and diminish the lunar influences we receive from the Zodiac.

As the Moon moves through its cycle the pressure it adds to the Moon sign's influence on our behavior varies considerably. The new Moon is at the beginning the lunar cycle. The added effect it has on the current Moon sign and on us will be in its initial stages, too. As the Moon waxes it adds pressure to the Moon sign, and the effect of the Moon sign on us will correspondingly increase. The influence of a new Cancer Moon may be weak, but as the Moon waxes to full, the Cancer Moon's influence will strengthen. Likewise, as the Moon wanes, the influence of the Cancer Moon or any Moon sign will weaken.

As the Moon waxes, its influence increases. Every day the Moon becomes a little stronger. Just because the Moon does not seem to have an effect on your emotions upon entering a new sign of the Zodiac, it does not mean that its effects will not manifest before the Moon goes void of course or leaves the sign.

The full Moon is the Moon's strongest position. Moon signs are most influential when the Moon is full. The Moon's passage through the signs of the Zodiac will be at its most dramatic and profound at this time. A full Pisces Moon might even cause the strong, unemotional type to shed a tear or two. A normally emotional person, with undue emotional stresses, might be so influenced by a full Pisces or Cancer Moon that their emotional outburst could very well lead to a total breakdown of emotional defenses, resulting in a flood of tears.

I have a lot of respect for the Water full Moons: Cancer, Scorpio, and Pisces. They have torn me apart on more than one occasion. One Cancer full Moon had me completely beside myself in tears for two days.

The waning Moon will have the opposite effect on the intensity of the Moon sign as the waxing Moon. It will decrease in intensity as the Moon wanes toward the dark Moon. The Moon's influence will be strongest as the Moon enters a new sign; you may feel some relief from its influences as it begins to go void of course.

The dark Moon will be a time of symbolic death and rejuvenation. Its influences will be along those lines. It will have an energy conducive to change. When the dark Moon arrives, you will most feel the need to make changes in your life. The type of change will depend on the sign the Moon is in and the depth at which the change needs to occur. The new and full Moons' energy is the same—it differs only in volume. The dark Moon's energy is altogether different. The darkness of the Moon leads us into the recesses of the inner-self. There we are instructed to examine what exists and make use of it in our daily lives. When our outer-self does not coincide with our inner-self, the dark Moon applies pressure to make changes. Such changes are good for us and make us whole. Pay close attention to your feelings during the dark Moon, for there is much to learn.

The personality shifts described in the twelve signs above are in many cases exaggerated. Everyone is different and no one thing affects two people in the same manner. Each person has their own emotional standards and personality traits in varying degrees of intensity. As the Moon passes through each of the twelve signs in the Zodiac, it influences the basic emotional and personality traits of each individual. Since each person starts with a different combination of basic traits, the lunar influences on these traits will be different as well.

The changes described above are also exaggerated to make it easier to see how the Moon will affect your emotions. If you're normally a very emotionally reserved individual, an intensely emotional Moon such as Cancer, Scorpio, or Pisces may cause you to smile all day or just seem a little sad; whereas if you were a highly emotional individual, a Water Moon might make you so joyful that others become annoyed or, like me, you could cry for two days straight. The difference is not the sign the Moon is in or even the Moon itself; the difference is found within you and how you react to lunar influences.

You will notice the effect the Moon has on your emotional state will go through periods of adjustment as your own emotional intensity and honesty varies. I have allowed myself to experience the Moon's influences and have grown immeasurably in my self-awareness. I know myself so much better than I ever had and become closer to my alter ego every day. As I have brought my ego-based personality, that which I show others, more in sync with my true self, my enjoyment of life has increased exponentially and my friendships are more intimate.

It is important to stay open to all that occurs. It's easy to shut down and refuse to experience your emotional life, but a big part of life will be missing if you do. If you start to believe there is nothing worthwhile in all of these emotional changes, you are letting your ego steal a very important and truly wonderful piece of your life.

Allow yourself to experience life. You will find it very enjoyable and, along the way, will learn something of yourself. You will learn who you really are. In doing so, you allow others to see your true self. This sounds scary but is really the best way to instill closeness and intimacy in your relationships.

Chapter 5

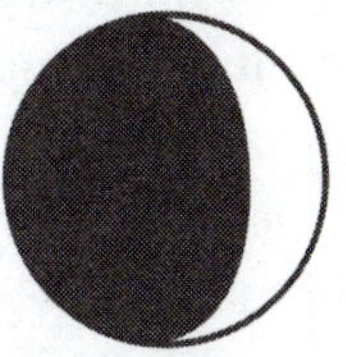

Moon Sign Characteristics

By getting in touch with the lunar energies that influence our lives, we can be better prepared to deal with the world on our terms. The physical changes that occur within our bodies are quite amazing and, at times, even unbelievable. The intensity of this physical phenomena is only surpassed by our emotional changes. We must also deal with the emotional states of others and the physical world around us, both of which are enormously influenced by the Moon. The ability to allow these celestial influences to work for us, rather than against us, is the result of understanding the emotional characteristics given each of us at birth and what effect cyclical lunar influences have on these basic characteristics.

You are about to embark on a journey. The success of this or any journey requires two basic things: a destination and a starting point. In this case, the destination is total self-awareness, and the starting point is the basic lunar personality. We must know where we are going or we will never arrive. A map only helps if your present location is known—the Moon's influence is our map, while your lunar sign is its key.

A lunar ephemeris, originally published in Grant Lewi's *Astrology for the Millions,* is provided in the appendix. The term "ephemeris" refers to a publication that lists the astrological positions of heavenly bodies throughout the year. In this case, the ephemeris refers only to the position of the Moon. Using your birth date, look up your Moon sign in the tables. You may need to know your birth time if the Moon changed signs on your birthday.

Now that you've discovered your Moon sign, compare your own birth traits with those discussed under each sign. You will probably find some similarities, though a few of them may be difficult to accept. Remember that each of us has our own unique mix of personality traits. The labels "good" and "bad" are determined within our own set of values and the perceptions of society. Life can be less complicated once we can honestly accept who we are without trying to hide a particular quality or feel guilty for doing so. Some people may try to hide their ability to nurture others; they deem this particular quality to be "bad" because they are afraid that it makes them appear to be weak and vulnerable. Others revel in their nurturing abilities because they feel that it is "good" to comfort others.

The twelve Zodiac signs are discussed separately in the following twelve sections. Each section will deal with the natal traits of a Moon sign, and, more specifically, the effect that the Moon's influence will have on your natal traits as the Moon passes through the twelve signs of the Zodiac.

The explanations offered in this chapter of an individual's emotional traits have in many cases been exaggerated for the purpose of clear understanding. You may or may not react exactly a described. There are nine other planets in your astrological chart—each of those planets has its own influence on you as it moves through the heavens on its cyclic journey. The Moon by far has the greatest influence on your emotional state and responses. The other planets may affect you differently, each of which may enhance or partially counteract the Moon's influence.

If you spend some time reading this information and comparing it to your own personality and emotional responses, you will have the opportunity to learn a great deal about yourself. The Moon influences your emotional personality (or inner-self). The inner-self is an amazingly powerful part of the soul, and by understanding it and its emotional responses to outside stimuli, you can harness this extreme power for your use and assistance in life.

Your lunar personality has a good deal to say about how you live and deal with others. By deepening your understanding of yourself, you also gain the ability to deepen your understanding of the relationships in your life. We deal with life in the same manner as we deal with relationships, and we deal with relationships as we deal with ourselves. To practice dealing with life and relationships is to learn about yourself.

This whole process is a journey of self-discovery. The real you, the subconscious part of you that controls everything you do, is awaiting an invitation to come out and play. By getting in touch with this elusive part of your mind, you will learn what is really important in your life and how to accentuate the positive. You will learn to recognize the negative aspects in your life as well, thus allowing yourself to lessen their effect on you. By boosting positive and reducing negative influences, you will convert your dreams into reality.

Aries Moon

Your Lunar Profile

Aries is the Zodiac's first sign. Aries is a Fire sign that is ruled by Mars (the god of war). This is a Masculine sign with lots of positive energy.

You are aggressive, energetic, dynamic, assertive, and very active. You easily express yourself and love a good adventure. Decision making comes naturally for you. The danger lies in making decisions without due consideration. Your strong intuition is offset by your impatience, which challenges you to get what you want out of life. Once on the hunt, you will go after your desires with dynamic passion. Taking second place to no one, you want to stand in the winner's circle right now, or sooner.

Enthusiasm and decisiveness make you a good leader. The success of long-term projects depends on the work of others as your focus changes quickly, and this can be irritating because you're very independent. Your Sun sign could have a great influence on your need to be immediately successful and your willingness to see things through.

Sudden outbursts of temper are not uncommon, but they rarely last long and disappear without a trace. You are independent and righteous, intolerant of interference, and though you can dominate an emotional relationship, your feelings are hurt easily. Self-absorption is a short walk for you, making it difficult for you to work well with others.

The Moon is Feminine. When her influence is combined with Aries' warlike ruler, you become unstoppable. Your aggressive behavior is supported by a deeply caring, deeply spiritual idealist. Beneath that rough exterior is a true romantic who can get involved in a relationship very quickly. You differ from an Aries Sun sign in that it is easier for others to see the romantic in you. This is due to the Moon's rulership by Cancer, a Water sign. Water dampens fire, and lessens the intensity of Aries' fiery approach to people, situations, and opportunities. You are very charming, and understand that life is for living. Overall, happiness is secured through a creative outlet of some kind.

The combination of Fire and Water is very positive. Cool, calming water helps to keep your hotter side under control, allowing your emotions to be dealt with honestly. You are outgoing and the life of the party. Depending on your other astrological aspects, the combination of Fire and Water elements could be rather volatile, and create an unstable love life. When an emotional upset does occur, you quickly deal with it and get past it.

Influences on the Aries Moon Personality

Aries Moon Personality in an Aries Moon

This is a period of intensity for you. Life will be very exciting with your dynamic energies and emotions running full speed. It wouldn't hurt to deliberately slow down your pace. Decisions made during one of these fast-paced, emotionally charged Moons could be based on misconceptions. An Aries Moon personality in an Aries Moon is typified with the phrase, "It is better to burn out than fade away." Be prepared to slow down as the Moon passes into Taurus.

Once I received what should have been a one hour massage in twenty minutes by an Aries Moon therapist in an Aries Moon. Not only did she have the fastest hands in the west, she spoke so quickly I could neither participate in the conversation nor relax.

Aries Moon Personality in a Taurus Moon

A few days of impatience is your struggle during this Moon. The Taurus Moon likes to do things one step at a time. With a highly energized personality like yours, the Taurus Moon will not drain you of energy, but it will provide a calming effect that is likely to be unappreciated by your normally active, impatient self. The Taurus Moon is grounding, and marks a time to direct your energies at home. Plan to take care of things that require an inward focus, more detail than speed, or steadfastness to complete. Starting a new project will be difficult. Gardening, reading, or even taking a nap are worthwhile activities in this Moon. Avoid activities that require lots of energy—you will be sluggish and unproductive. Avoid too many group activities or relationship issues because you will be intolerant of others as well as of yourself. Back off a little and try to keep your life in proper perspective as you enter the Gemini Moon.

Aries Moon Personality in a Gemini Moon

There will be a certain duality of the self during this Moon. You could have a tendency to talk endlessly and rationalize your feelings. You will feel a need to couple your spiritual beliefs with your mental processes. If your spiritual beliefs spur a desire to develop a deeper understanding of life's mysteries, this is a time to learn and to bring your life into balance. If you are not up to the challenge, you could begin to question your beliefs, thus causing an imbalance. This scenario can be played out in many different aspects of life. The Gemini Moon is a time of affirmation and confirmation if your life is well balanced and properly structured to benefit your lifelong goals. This is also a time of confusion, if the rewards of your work don't feed your soul.

Reuben, a computer salesperson with an Aries Moon, is extremely talkative on and off the job, but is especially dramatic in Air Moons. The Gemini Moon not only enhances his communication skills, it helps him to voice his feelings. Quite often he makes statements that reveal his emotional insecurities. Reuben will seldom talk of the happier or gentler side of life.

Balance is the key word of the Gemini Moon. A positive, balanced outlook will be helpful going into the Cancer Moon.

Aries Moon Personality in a Cancer Moon

This is a time of emotional mystery. The Cancer Moon can be an emotional roller coaster—it influences you to allow yourself as much self-imposed happiness or misery as you wish. While the Cancer Moon goes about its regular duties, tempting your emotions to come out and play, your Aries energy will intensify all that occurs. The mood swings you experience will not seem to belong to you, and you may have difficulty coping with them. The Cancer Moon is a mysterious place for you because you don't understand these changing moods or their origin. You don't normally deal well with the changing moods of others. Since you don't understand the mood swings you're experiencing, you won't deal well with these, either. The best course of action is to come into this Moon with a well-balanced outlook on life. The Cancer Moon can be a fun time if you have been honest about your feelings. The Cancer Moon and emotional honesty go hand in hand. Regardless of how you feel now, the Leo Moon, with some familiar fiery energy, is just around the corner.

Aries Moon Personality in a Leo Moon

Leo's fiery energy doesn't feel exactly like home, but it is close. Aries and Leo Moons can be in conflict, because each wants to control the emotional self. In this Moon you will feel more domineering. You are happy and attracted to this Moon's energy, but be careful not to instantaneously combust from the compatible yet dissimilar fiery influences at work here.

Your basic lunar traits will be accentuated; the Leo Moon brings dominance to the picture. This isn't necessarily a bad thing. You need to control your emotions after the Cancer Moon sets them free. Your Aries side will want to put any emotional upheaval in the past and move forward, while the Leo Moon will try to take control of your emotions. This is effective if you have a situation that requires more courage than emotional involvement. After all, this Moon brings the courage and strength of the Lion. If you've made a decision that requires action, you would be well advised to take action now, because the coming Virgo Moon will bring insecurity.

Aries Moon Personality in a Virgo Moon

The earthly qualities of this Moon could bring your quick movement to a slow walk. You are an emotional creature, set off by outside influences, and this particular earthly influence will cause you to second-guess all you're considering at the moment and possibly overanalyze the situation. This isn't a good time to make decisions unless the situation is very detailed and requires a sharp analytical mind. Overanalysis breeds insecurity during Virgo Moons.

Aries Moon Personality in the Libra Moon

Fire cannot exist without oxygen, which explains its attraction to Air. In the Zodiac, the Libra Moon is your opposite, and opposites do attract. Your innate charm will emerge, while your fiery side, which causes others to take a step back, will be subdued.

You are a true romantic, and this Moon will allow that side of you to shine. This is a good time to work on your love life. Open yourself to the energy of this Moon, because it can balance your life inside and out. Watch how differently people react in this Moon compared to other, less congenial Moons. This is the Moon that best suits your overall happiness. Maintain this happiness and balance as long as you can.

Aries Moon Personality in the Scorpio Moon

This is a very sensual, passionate time. In fact, the word "passion" sums up your emotional responses—you are drawn to others, especially the opposite sex. The light of your flame is drawn into the darkness, but doesn't provide enough light to make you comfortable. The Scorpio Moon is about attraction to the hidden. You want what you cannot see and are jealous of those who receive anything you might want. If you can keep your jealousy in check, this is a very sexual time. Your Aries energy adds to the passion provided by the Scorpion, but remember that the Scorpion consumes her mate. Your intense emotional energy may lead you to be too passionate about your needs and goals. Listen to your gut feelings when you're cautious or reluctant. Enjoy this lusty feeling and allow it to take you happily into the next Moon.

Aries Moon Personality in the Sagittarius Moon

Optimism and cheerfulness are characteristics of this Moon. The familiar fiery energy makes you feel good. This is a time to go with what makes you happy. This is not a time for structure or rigidity. Actually, I've never met an Aries Moon personality that's comfortable with either.

Live for the moment and let life take you where it wants to go. If you try to fight the flow, you will meet with great resistance. It's ill-advised to work on solving problems, heavily emotional subjects, details, or any structured task. You will quickly become resentful of the chains that these place upon you. If you must work against the Sagittarius Moon's energies, know you will be tempted to stray from the task at hand.

Aries Moon Personality in the Capricorn Moon

This Moon is very grounded. You will be more rational than you like to be, and the strength of this Moon will be hard to overcome. This is an excellent time to make decisions. The tendency to overanalyze is not present—just cool, calm, rational thought. This can be irritating, however, because you are a person of action. Take advantage of this Moon by using it to plan and make decisions. Trust your feelings. From this point of view, life will appear to be just the way you like it: a series of battles in which victory shines as a message to all. Plan your next conquest and you will be well served when this transit is over.

Aries Moon Personality in the Aquarius Moon

This is the time for the warrior to emerge. This isn't a Moon for emotional commitment. Your detachment from the outcome and from others will prove to be a challenge for your normally emotional self, but is of great benefit when victory is essential.

Your need to impetuously move forward, coupled with cool pitilessness, can easily incense others. The Aquarian Moon is best used to work on difficult stresses where your emotions block your progress. The detachment you have from your own emotions will help you to break through some of those emotional barriers. Your sense of detachment under this Moon's influence can be of assistance. Your need for a challenge can be met while focusing on the source of your emotional blocks rather than on possible results.

Aries Moon Personality in the Pisces Moon

Your truly romantic side will come out during this Moon without the usual dynamic energy you so often display. This Water Moon will also improve your psychic and intuitive abilities, and make it easier to understand the feelings of others. The danger is in allowing the emotions of others to affect your feelings. You are very sympathetic and your emotions are heightened during this Moon. You look for the romance of life. If you plan on watching a tear-jerking movie during these few days, be sure to take along a box of tissues. This is a good time for heartfelt gestures and deep conversations. Experience and enjoy the romance that you are so adept at creating. Solitude or spending time with people whose emotions are in full swing will have a tremendous effect on your emotional balance.

Taurus Moon

Your Lunar Profile

Taurus is a Feminine, Earth sign. Those born with this Moon sign are prone to stubbornness, great willpower, and materialism. The Taurus Moon is ruled by Venus, the goddess of love.

One natal influence of the Taurus Moon will be to keep you firmly grounded. You are a practical individual, able to save money and care for financial affairs with ease. It's possible to have anything you want in the material world, and most of it will be beautiful.

You are dependable and strong. Inner strength and willpower help you to achieve your goals, once underway. You are quite energetic, and your storehouse of energy seldom seems to dwindle. Between your high level of energy and intense willpower, you are an awesome force. There is a danger of getting carried away with your power. For all of the strength and energy you possess, you need the prodding of another to get started. Once moving you are very hard to stop, but getting you started can be a chore in itself.

You are quite emotionally reserved. Others will push your buttons without effect; however, once you reach your limit, your wrath cuts loose like a dam breaking. It is best to stand out of your way. Venus, as a ruler, imparts a very sensitive side to you. All who are close to you know that they are cared for deeply. When with the one you love, you are apt to introduce romance into your relationship. You always strive to be well groomed and mannerly, and expect your companion to do the same. What attracts you most to a mate initially are beauty, status, and the bottom line. Ultimately, you will only marry if you have a deep bond, and have discovered your true soul mate.

The search for this soul mate can lead to uncertainty. You may be unwilling to commit to anyone unless convinced that he or she is "the one." You have the ability to sit and wait but most people do not. Care must be taken not to overlook the other person's feelings. You are a very caring soul but your stubbornness sometimes overshadows everything.

You have the ability to calm the most irritated, angry individual. The calm, grounded person that everyone sees is one of the best sedatives for emotional upheaval. Your friends call you when things go wrong because your sensitive, caring nature and calm attitude helps them to see the real problems. Conversely, when things are not going well for you or when you are introduced into unfamiliar situations, you withdraw.

Security and stability are your main desires in life. From this basis, you can achieve anything. You like your home to feel secure because it's your sanctuary when times are tough. A stable lifestyle is important to you in this world of constant change. You depend on your home life as the one area of consistency. On the flip side, you don't cope with change well. Maintaining the status quo is most comfortable for you.

Influences on the Taurus Moon Personality

Taurus Moon Personality in the Aries Moon

The Fire of this Moon will definitely get your motor running. The sedate Taurus Moon needs some help getting started, and this may be the energy that you need. Start something new during this Moon.

Aries is a very passionate sign and could very easily stir up lustful feelings. Go with it, and have some fun. You need not worry as your desire for stability will keep you from getting too involved until the time is right.

Work can be dealt with in a similar manner. Try a new approach or take on a new project. These fiery days are just what you need to get things well underway.

Taurus Moon Personality in the Taurus Moon

This is a really comfortable Moon for you. It is the natal energy you have been dealing with all your life, so you probably feel energized and secure. Happiness is a result of being in your home. You may notice that while this Moon feels good, it might be too comfortable.

This Moon is best used for getting things done, and to complete projects which have already been started. It is also a good time to deal with difficult, emotion-laced problems. Your sense of logic will shine through any fog.

One Taurus Moon person I know, Joseph, is very energetic during this Moon but only in the intellectual and emotional realms. He can talk to his wife all day and night about his feelings, but doesn't think to take out the trash.

Taurus Moon Personality in the Gemini Moon

This is a good Moon to work on cognitive efforts. The sharp intellect of the Gemini Moon will be of benefit in making discoveries. When an unsolved situation persists, use the energies of this Moon to try new approaches toward finding a solution. Gemini is an Air Moon and will go in many directions at once. The stability of your natal Moon, Taurus, will partially negate this airy energy. There is too little stability here to make new long-term plans. Use its energies to find new directions along existing paths. To embark on a journey in this Moon would certainly spell defeat, because this Moon is not focused and stable enough for your tastes.

Taurus Moon Personality in the Cancer Moon

The stability of your home life is an essential place of escape in the Cancer Moon. Your base is your home, and your home must be a place of security for you to be happy. If your home is a secure, happy place then this Moon will be happy time for you. Use it to look honestly at your self. This can be a positive learning experience and much easier to deal with than a negative one.

The Taurus Moon personality reacts slowly to emotional discontent. Where emotions are concerned, you are like the tortoise. You move slowly and steadily, experiencing all that life has to offer. Difficulties arise because the very nature of emotions requires their immediate expression. The Cancer Moon helps to speed emotional responses. My friend Sara often had not dealt with her emotions when the Cancer Moon came around—she was hammered by the sudden onslaught.

If your home life is not as stable as you would like it to be, you may be in for a ride during this Moon. A Cancer Moon will strip you of the barriers you've built between the world and your inner-self. The emotions that surface are true and honest, but they have been stuffed inside for too long and want you to know about it. Again, this is a great learning experience, so keep your mind open. You not only learn how you are reacting to the world's stimuli, you will also learn to accept and experience emotions when they first show up rather than swallowing them.

Taurus Moon Personality in the Leo Moon

This is another Fire sign that can add a little pick-me-up to life. The Leo Moon has a rather flamboyant energy. Leo has as much willpower as Taurus, but isn't as stubborn. You can use this Leo Moon energy to feed your intentions. This is a good time to make some progress toward your goals. It also a good time to deal with emotional situations which require a certain amount of nobility, or a calm yet intense energy. Sara loves this Moon as its warming energy helps her to dry out after the Cancer Moon. This is an energy that intimidates.

Look inside yourself. This is a nice sunny time to work on improving your self-image. To the practical Taurus Moon persona, a dramatic expression of self-love might seem a little ridiculous, but it is often these self-dramatizations that help us to get the message. Take care of yourself during this Moon by doing something special. Your nobility deserves some recognition.

Taurus Moon Personality in the Virgo Moon

A good earthy look at your relationship with yourself is in order. In this Moon, "work" is the key word. The analytical side of Virgo will certainly help in that respect, by allowing you to see the little things you do to sabotage your ability to get what you really want. Since you are at home in this earthy energy, there's enough support to tackle anything that needs work, such as your image, appearance, personal goals, purpose in life, or successes and failures. Examine what is working for you and what is not.

This applies to your relationships, too. The way you treat others is an indicator of how you treat yourself. By improving the relationships around you, you will automatically be improving your relationship with yourself.

If you decide not to take advantage of this Moon's analytical disposition for self-examination, the Virgo Moon will point out the details of your personality and your relationships that need work. There will be lots of criticism, analyzing, and self-judgment. Stay away from this destructive cycle.

Taurus Moon Personality in the Libra Moon

A couple of days of indecision never hurts anyone. The Libra Moon is an Air Moon, and it will allow others to easily influence you. This contradiction will show up in your life as indecision, since you are usually very decisive after proper deliberation.

Joseph is very methodical when it comes to making decisions and purchases. During this Moon, Joseph's usually slow pace becomes even slower, primarily due to indecision. He goes through a process of weighing all the factors, unless materialistic urges are at work, in which case he becomes rather impulsive.

This Moon will intensify your desire for a peaceful, loving relationship with yourself and those around you. You will shy away from conflict in favor of the harmonious areas in your life. Look to the relationship that offers the most loving atmosphere and hide out there for a few days. Continue to work on relationships that need harmony and love. This peaceful Moon will provide ample opportunity to bring beauty and love into your life and the lives of those around you.

Taurus Moon Personality in the Scorpio Moon

The emotions that arise during this Moon can range from sensuality to lustful desire. The Scorpio Moon is opposed to the Taurus Moon and, as such, there is a powerful attraction here. The Scorpio Moon's deeply arousing qualities will inspire your own sense of carnal desire. This Moon is famous for increasing sensual feelings in all the signs of the Zodiac, so don't feel like you've been singled out. Let go of that practical side and enjoy the passion.

These lustful feelings could make you susceptible to jealousy. Remember, you are not the only person being affected—other people's jealousy could flare up as well. You will be well-advised to stop flirting with anyone but your mate. A fiery Sagittarius Moon follows, and unresolved jealousy in that Moon could spell trouble.

Taurus Moon Personality in the Sagittarius Moon

The Fire energy of Sagittarius can produce a very happy time. The difficulty is in letting it happen. Your practical, rather sedate, nature will hold you back from enjoying the moment if your actions don't immediately appear beneficial or thought-provoking. The ability to let go and play is elusive in Taurus Moon people, but very important and worth the effort.

This Moon provides the perfect opportunity to nurture your religious beliefs without the risk of deep emotional turmoil. The Sagittarius Moon also provides a childlike opportunity for idealistic, emotional attachments. The child in you surfaces in many ways. If you don't help this inner child to express itself in a beneficial manner, it will choose its own form of self-expression.

Taurus Moon Personality in the Capricorn Moon

This Earth sign will boost your innate need for stability and security, and will drive you to tie up loose ends. The emotional arena will be quiet as you withdraw.

The Taurus Moon personality can be lazy, but the Capricorn Moon will encourage and direct your efforts. Your hard work is best directed toward improving your financial security and your status within your community and work group. This Moon emphasizes achievement for the sake of personal financial security. To work at a project which is nothing more than busy work or in which you have no personal stake will be fruitless. You will quickly become disinterested and move on to something else.

Emotionally, you will appear withdrawn. Avoid emotional withdrawal by pushing yourself to be more outgoing. Security and your financial world are on your mind right now. Once the stubborn Taurus is focused, change is difficult.

Taurus Moon Personality in the Aquarius Moon

This is another unemotional Moon that fosters emotional withdrawal. In this Moon, however, you will be friendly to others, and better able to carry on a conversation. You will not be willing to let others see the real you, and in that respect, you are still withdrawn and impersonal. The intentions of others are important but you don't necessarily trust their motives.

Although you are emotionally fortified and won't let others in, you are compassionate towards those who are less fortunate. Helping others will ultimately help you include others in your life. The Aquarius Moon is known for its intuitive insights, and making use of these insights is beneficial. This is still a productive time, so trust your intuition to take the next step forward.

Taurus Moon Personality in the Pisces Moon

Your empathy will be turned up during this Moon. Understanding the feelings of others will have an effect on your own emotions. Don't be surprised if you feel the urge to shed a tear or two.

Romance is one of the things you appreciate most, and this Moon provides the perfect opportunity. The urge to pursue your romantic desires will be great and should be followed. Try not to get caught up in issues of security. Romantic interludes are not by nature emotionally secure. This lack of security could cause unnecessary, self-imposed isolation. Be wary of your real motivations when you feel yourself pulling away. Force yourself to experience your desires.

Since you are empathically open to the world in this Moon, and your feelings of security are not at their peak, you may feel defenseless and far too accessible. Your feelings may be easily hurt. Your imagination is also running at full speed right now, so what you perceive may not necessarily be the truth. Take it easy on yourself.

Gemini Moon

Your Lunar Profile

Your basic personality is that of an intelligent, imaginative, extrovert who loves to banter. You are prone to talk incessantly, and to switch from topic to topic on a whim.

Your mind is quite active and full of imaginative ideas. When you take advantage of your quick-wittedness and inherent, creative resourcefulness, few can keep up with your mental agility. Others will not consider focus and concentration to be your strong points. They assume that your ability to jump so quickly from one subject to another is a sign of impatience. These perceptions can be true, but only when you have too many things to do, because you try and squeeze them all into your work schedule.

Intuition is a key factor when dealing with others. One of the reasons that you are so quick-witted is that you have an instinctual ability to dissect a situation and react, and your first reaction is usually correct.

You are an exciting person to be around. Mercury, the planet of communication, is the ruler of Gemini. This gives you very good communication skills. You are a skilled conversationalist and a natural interrogator. You may ask many personal questions that delve deep into another's private matters while being unwilling to reciprocate. When your conversations are filled with quick wit and a rapidly changing focus, be aware of your capriciousness and flirtatiousness. Others may begin to distrust you, especially if gossiping becomes a vice.

You have the ability to look at your inner-self and rationally diagnose your emotional situation. This honesty is an admirable trait; however, you might make conclusions based on delusions or distortions of the truth, depending on your intuitive ability and level of trust in that ability. You are a very fun person, and a lively conversationalist. Practice heartfelt communication and emotional spontaneity in your conversations, reduce the emphasis on charm and wit, and target your focus on others.

Influences on the Gemini Moon Personality

Gemini Moon Personality in the Aries Moon

This could be a difficult combination for you. The heat of the Aries Moon will intensify the emotions you keep so well hidden. You may feel like you are going to explode. You will have a quicker temper than usual and will be less able to analyze the source of emotional turmoil.

Your quick wit may be a little more pointed and direct. The fiery aspect of the Aries Moon will add heat and energy to your emotional repertoire. Try to channel this energy into some form of productive work not requiring a great deal of analysis. Personal interludes may go awry.

Gemini Moon Personality in the Taurus Moon

In this Moon you may find yourself uncharacteristically sedate. Your quick repartee may be slow, and your outgoing personality withdrawn. Others will not notice the change in you, but for you this grounding feels like a ball and chain.

Sammy's wife, Becca, is intensely influenced by the Earth Moons. According to Becca, she lacks her usual enthusiastic motivation in the Taurus Moon, and feels sluggish. I don't see the difference in her, but she feels it.

Emotionally, you will be more practical in your approach, and more sensitive to others' needs and emotions. The Taurus Moon is a sensitive, caring Moon, and its influence should affect you in a similar manner. Because your normal state is to be mentally quick and emotionally negligent, your own emotions may become more susceptible to injury. The risk of being subjected to emotional injury is not new to you, but it seldom happens. Your inner-self is kept deep within, and to suddenly have it subjected to examination may be a little frightening for you.

Gemini Moon Personality in the Gemini Moon

The Gemini Moon will magnify your already outgoing personality. You will feel at home with these energies, though possibly frustrated from lack of concentration. Even the most unfocused personality can become too unfocused. You will be unusually flighty. Try to put a short-term damper on any changes in relationships or domiciles. Care must be taken if you are to make any progress during this Moon. This includes progress at work as well as in relationships. With the ability to engage your friends and associates with your quick wit, you will really have to be careful now.

This is a fantastic time to work on the creative aspects of life. Imagination and creativity are two personality traits that will work overtime. Take advantage of the positive aspects of the Gemini Moon's energy.

Gemini Moon Personality in the Cancer Moon

This Water Moon shouldn't be much trouble. You will recognize the emotional changes brought on by this Moon and will quickly react to minimize their effect. Although the Cancer Moon will dominate your emotional responses to the outside world, you won't stay focused long enough to be ill-affected by this Moon's emotional honesty. This would be a good time to pursue introspection, if you are up to it. There is the possibility that long-hidden issues will force their way to the surface. In that case, the Cancer Moon will certainly help you to open up and deal with them. Honesty about your feelings makes the task easier.

The Cancer Moon provides some domestic energy along with introspection. This could be a good time to take care of those household duties that you have been ignoring: scrub the oven, clean out the garage, or maybe even tackle the closets.

Gemini Moon Personality in the Leo Moon

The Leo Moon will add fizz to your already bubbly personality. You will desire recognition and have a flare for the dramatic, but will only display your emotions in a spotlight. These emotional dramatics can be a stretch for the Gemini Moon personality—the outer persona could handle the drama easily, but to bring the inner-self into the play might be difficult. At any rate, your emotional world will heat up. You will probably find the intensity of the spotlight agreeable, but backpedaling may start with an emotional commitment. Provocative behavior may invite trouble. If the situation between you and another becomes extreme, you might consider backing off. When the Leo Moon's energy returns fire with fire, life gets complicated very quickly.

Gemini Moon Personality in the Virgo Moon

Two communicative giants at work together might describe, with little exaggeration, this Moon's influence on you. Virgo's skill in communication is natural because the Virgo Moon is ruled by Mercury. Your intellect will be bolstered by this Moon but, more importantly, your staying power will be increased; that is, if you open yourself to the Moon's influences. You are likely to rely on the tenacity of the Virgo Moon to take on bigger tasks than you could normally handle. If you are involved with projects requiring real focus and hard work, you cannot pick a better time to complete them. However, you could become bored with a monotonous project after a short time, and drop it for something that promises excitement. If a task doesn't hold your attention, don't bother with it; you will only feel guilty about quitting. Watch for critical behavior and compulsive analysis of details as warning signs that you are becoming disenchanted with the work at hand. You must moderate Virgo's energy in order to use it—moderation requires control.

Gemini Moon Personality in the Libra Moon

This Moon is an Air Moon that is more indecisive and possessive than your natal Moon. Indecisiveness in a Libra Moon is exaggerated and becomes the primary personality trait. Your indecisiveness probably won't affect important decisions, but will influence trivial matters such as what to have for dinner, what clothes to wear, what household chore to work on first, or what television channel to watch. These are the kinds of things that make you and others crazy.

The influences of the Libra Moon should be familiar as they are similar in nature to the Gemini Moon, but with a greater sense of fairness. Life must be in balance. Spend some time with your primary relationship. If you have not found that special person, you will wish you had.

Your charm will be working for you in this Moon, and this is a good time to socialize. I don't see Sammy very often but when he does invite me to join him and Becca, it is usually in an Air Moon.

You will be successful in dealing with matters concerning the public, because your instincts will be keen. Your sense of fairness keeps them coming back. Be very cognizant of your tendency to stretch the truth. You will be found out immediately, and lose credibility. This is a Moon of justice.

Gemini Moon Personality in the Scorpio Moon

"Passion in all things" is the key phrase of this Water Moon. Your intensity will grow during this Moon. You will find it hard to keep those well-hidden emotions in check. Your physical and romantic desires will go into full swing, as your flirtations become more serious. Emotional desires will also bring up other emotions. Resign yourself to dealing with these feelings and be prepared to experience their effect. Make peace with them or they will vex you.

Be careful that your innate charm, bolstered by this Moon, does not turn to a poisonous sting if you run into difficulties in achieving your goals. You will find that your temper is on edge. You are passionate about your desires and willing to negotiate a fair settlement.

The Scorpio Moon has a very direct energy when dealing with others and a secretive desire when dealing with the self. It's harder to open your inner-self to examination but self-examination is essential to a healthy soul.

Gemini Moon Personality in the Sagittarius Moon

You will feel peppy, joyful and relaxed during this Fire Moon. Your courageous self-examination in the Scorpio Moon has been emotionally rewarding; now it is time to be idealistic. It's best to continue to have fun with your life's companion since you are still attracted to this connective energy. Watch yourself closely for signs of impatience and insensitive behavior. Stumble now and you will be called on your actions. This fiery Moon can provoke a heated response. Avoid simple friendships and play in the passion of the Sagittarius Moon. It's not as emotionally draining as the Scorpio Moon and will be more fun.

Gemini Moon Personality in the Capricorn Moon

Your flighty personality will be accompanied by mood swings as you pass through this Earth Moon. Financial and emotional security in life will become a priority. The lack of either will bring depression. This is grounded energy, possibly too grounded for the fast moving Gemini Moon.

The weight of this grounded Capricorn energy may be too much for the productive lunar Gemini. When feeling lethargic, rest and recuperate. You are just not up to life speed while wearing these concrete Capricorn shoes. The solution is to slow down and take care of yourself. If you need a little security, open a savings account.

Gemini Moon Personality in the Aquarius Moon

The airy Aquarius Moon will feel good to you, and your basic traits will shine. The biggest challenge facing you is to maintain contact with your inner-self. The Aquarius Moon excels at keeping your emotions under control.

Your ability to reason will seldom be challenged in an Air Moon, but intelligence is not all there is to life. Peace with the inner-self and the ability to react to and display your emotions are what truly matter. In order to connect with people you must be honest with them, and to do that you must be honest with yourself.

Since you are on safe ground in this Aquarius Moon, let go of some emotional control and really connect to another person. The experience will be so rewarding that you will want to do it again. Your flamboyance puts you on center stage. By allowing emotions to show, you will be able to stay on stage, especially with intimate relationships that develop because of your willingness to share.

Gemini Moon Personality in the Pisces Moon

Pisces is the last of the Water Moons in the Zodiac. It will probably be a fairly dull Moon that does not add much in the way of adventure. The serene nature of the Pisces Moon can be joyful and relaxing if you let it. You are so rarely at rest that you may have to shift gears and slow down to the pace of this Moon. Enjoy life; you deserve a break.

Along the way, you will be warm and tender, and show genuine affection to those you love. Pisces is a sentimental Moon and this will reflect in your emotions and actions. Warm up and turn on the romance. You and your significant other will discover new common ground. It's all right if things get a little corny, because this is a quixotic Moon. If the romance becomes too perfect, all the better. Coincidentally, Sammy and Becca became engaged during a Pisces Moon. I can't think of a more perfect time for those two friends to have made a romantic commitment.

Cancer Moon

Your Lunar Profile

Cancer is the fourth sign of the Zodiac. It is ruled by the Moon, and is a Feminine, Water sign. Although the Moon is not a planet, its influence is as great as the planets in astrology. If you are a person born with a Cancer Moon, you are very nurturing, compassionate, and caring. You often put others' needs before your own.

You can be very moody. Since you are sensitive to the actions and reactions of others, your mood can change as quickly as the wind. This sensitivity is enhanced by your extreme psychic awareness. Emotional insecurity is another reason for your quick mood changes.

I have several friends born with their Moon in Cancer. Each of them has one trait common to the others—they react quickly and emotionally to changes around them. How my friends ultimately deal with emotional changes after their initial reaction is unique to each of them, but their immediate response is characteristically Cancerian.

When things are working for you, you are a nurturing parent, a trusted friend, and a compassionate mate. You enjoy your home, which is a source of security. If life should take a momentary turn for the worse, you can become overly sensitive, tearful, manipulating, insecure, and withdrawn. You may manipulate others through martyrdom—you are not above using tears to make others feel guilty.

Financial security is an issue for you, especially early in your career and near its end. In midlife you may be more concerned with bringing back the days of youth and indulging your every whim.

Emotional security is your biggest challenge. Trusting another to hold your heart is very difficult for you. Others must prove themselves over and over. The superpsychic abilities you possess help you greatly in sizing up another's personality. The rub comes from your being overly sensitive to other people's opinions of you. Others can hurt your feelings without malicious intent, or any intent at all. The trick is to learn the difference between psychic messages and emotional sensitivity.

Develop your latent psychic abilities by working with them. A little practice and effort will go a long way. Other Moon signs need to work much harder to develop that which you need only bring into consciousness.

The phases of the Moon have a tremendous effect on your emotional stability. The Moon rules Cancer—as the ruler changes so does its subjects. It would not be surprising to find that the intensity of your moods follows the cycle of the Moon: an incorrigibly upbeat mood around the full Moon, and an incredibly depressed mood during the new Moon. The dark Moon might easily pull you into a cave to withdraw from life for a while, like a crab into its shell.

Of course, the strength of these phases will vary, depending on the signs they are in. The Water signs are the strongest and Cancer tops them all. Your best course of action is to become intimate with your inner-self, in order to be an ally rather than an enemy of your emotions. Your susceptibility to others is like a psychic sponge—you soak up everything around you, both good and bad. Through meditation, you can place floodgates in your raging river of emotions, thus stabilizing their flow.

Influences on the Cancer Moon Personality

Cancer Moon Personality in the Aries Moon

This Fire Moon could bring some passion to your life. Your enthusiastic approach will undoubtedly brighten the days of the people in your life. The heat from this Moon will ignite a sexual ember within you.

The right partner could fan this ember into a flame. As with any fire, the hotter it burns, the faster it dies; however, instead of the Aries Moon burning itself out, watery Cancer will dampen the flames and cool the passion should it become too intense.

Aries adds a proportionate amount of recklessness to your personality. Again, this could be short-lived. The desire for security in all parts of your life will veto any ideas about "living fast and loose."

If your emotional self should be negatively influenced and take a turn for the worse, don't chastise yourself about passionate interludes or living in the fast lane. You will probably be angry with yourself, and feel that a self-inflicted caning might be your next order of business. Hopefully, you will avoid self-imposed torture, and accept who you are and how you react to things. A little self-acceptance and self-approval will go a long way toward promoting your happiness.

Cancer Moon Personality in the Taurus Moon

Taurus is the first of the Earth Moons, and will feel very good to you. The well-grounded Taurus Moon will greatly help to smooth out the rough spots in your emotional swings. Its pull is so great that you may not be able to reach the highest of emotional highs, but you won't sink to the depths, either.

Another Taurean trait is the desire for security, which is a good fit for you as well. This materialistic Moon wants the household to be a safe and secure haven—a place to return to after a day in the trenches. Its familiar energy and calming effect should be conducive to improving the self-image. Amy, a friend with a Cancer Moon, and I cleared the air between us through some heartfelt conversations during the Taurus Moon. Safety was not an issue because we both felt secure within ourselves.

Passion is a Taurean trait, though not as fiery as in the Aries Moon. In Taurus, passion and sensuality smolder together and slowly build to a comfortable flame. Take this opportunity to make something special happen in your life. Don't think this "passion" only applies to sex, either. Make it work for you.

Cancer Moon Personality in the Gemini Moon

If nothing else comes from this Air Moon, you should at least have a laugh or two. The many faces of Gemini will keep you guessing about your commitments as your concentration will be a bit off. At least the focus will not be on yourself.

The relationship between the Gemini Moon and the Cancer Moon personality was pleasurably demonstrated to me on a clear, warm, winter afternoon in San Francisco. Ariel and I were totally engaged in conversation on a deck overlooking the ocean. We drank a beer and laughed under heavy woolen blankets as the Sun set over the Pacific horizon. Later that evening, under the Gemini Moon, we walked to dinner, engulfed in each other's company.

You will continue to be intuitive during the Gemini Moon, but on an intellectual level. The Gemini intellect is very bright. When these forces are combined with your intuition, the result will be very productive, assuming that you are working on a short-term project. The airy influence of this Moon will not allow you to make a detailed analysis. Instead, you are like a murder investigator, who looks for clues to solve the case and relies on intuition to find them.

The opportunity for gaiety is upon you, especially if you can laugh at yourself when your mood is spiraling downward. If laughter fails and you start to decline toward depression, loosen your grip.

Cancer Moon Personality in the Cancer Moon

This Water Moon will mark your highest highs and your lowest lows. Everything you feel will be intensified. If you were to look in a mirror you might see etched in the glass, "Objects in the mirror are closer than they appear." You may not realize how emotional you may become in this Moon until you are in the heat of battle. You know yourself pretty well, but be extra careful around the new and full Moons.

Amy bounced with excitement during conversations which on another day would be fairly commonplace. Her double Cancerian influence helped to transform a normal day into an extraordinary experience.

If you remain positive about life, you may find that romance is in the air (or, should I say, water). A partner who likes the security of the home and hearth might make a firm impression on your heart. Love is a wonderful thing, but be cautious enough to listen to your instincts. You could get so caught up in the passion of the moment that you overlook who the object of your affection really is. Trust your inner-self. If your first impression tells you to move on, start packing. Your intuition is your first and best line of defense. When the bell rings, see who it is before you open the door.

Cancer Moon Personality in the Leo Moon

The Leo Moon can be relied upon to add some sunshine to dark and cloudy days. This Moon's energies are on the pushy side. You might find that you put yourself in charge of situations where you normally might not, or delegate work that you would usually just accept. This feeling of control over your life is very attractive to you. Many times you've felt no control over your emotional swings and reactions, but in the Leo Moon you will find some assertiveness that really warms the heart. Go with it and have a good time.

If your mood should start to turn, the Leo Moon's energy will turn right with you. Although protecting you from reaching the lower end of the scale, bossy Leo can negatively influence your mood. Complaints and criticisms could be your weapons when dealing with others.

Remember that, above all, the proud Lion is courageous. Don't be afraid to honestly look into the depths of your soul. You might find some of the answers you seek.

Cancer Moon Personality in the Virgo Moon

The Virgo Moon is known for its critical nature. This is a nit-picking Moon that relies on mental dexterity. Its emotions are usually grounded and it is not easily upset. You may find yourself worrying over some domestic detail which a few days ago would not have bothered you.

It is easy to criticize others, but can you accept the same from them, or from yourself? Look inward and understand that no one is perfect. You are honest enough with yourself to understand that this applies to you. Due to your sensitivity to the opinions of others, their criticism of you can become an emotional disaster. To avoid such complications, you might try to set an example for others by deliberately overlooking details and by concentrating on the positive elements of others' performances. You could encourage them to do their best and compliment what they have completed. It's much more difficult for others to criticize your efforts or appearance when you only display pride and pleasure with them.

A series of classes I attended stressed the importance of giving others "gifts of confidence"—truthful compliments given without expectation of return. The idea is to develop intimacy with others by bolstering their self-esteem, while allowing yourself to be vulnerable. I practice this regularly and feel wonderful when I see others respond to my "gifts."

Cancer Moon Personality in the Libra Moon

This is another Air Moon during which life should be tranquil. Libra is known for its indecisive behavior. Your emotional levels will be steady for the next couple of days. With all of this emotional freedom, you may feel that you can afford a romantic interlude. Something simple will do; if you try to plan an elaborate weekend away you will probably run headlong into indecision.

What do I want for dinner? Where shall I go on my walk? What should I do next? Which should I do first? Which program should I watch on TV? These are simple questions, but in this Moon, you may find it difficult to choose. This turns out to be more of an annoyance than anything else. If a really important choice should arise, your basic instincts will take over and the decision will be made in your usual manner. It's the little things that take too much energy.

This should be a good opportunity for some "R and R": relaxation and romance. My girlfriend and I spent a weekend together under the Libra Moon that turned out to be both relaxing and romantic. We couldn't decide on anything specific so we just let go: we slept late, went on short walks for coffee and longer walks for sunsets, talked endlessly, and enjoyed whatever the moment had to offer.

Cancer Moon Personality in the Scorpio Moon

The Scorpio Moon is an extremely emotional Water Moon. The emotional intensity of this Moon, coupled with your psychic abilities, will profoundly affect your basic emotional personality and should make for an intense journey. Prepare for the worst and hope for the best. You will probably do just fine unless you find yourself in a conflict. Should this occur, be careful, watch how you respond to others, use your intuition, and gauge what is being said to you. They may not be trying to hurt your feelings, but you are very sensitive. The Scorpio Moon can add directness and insensitivity when provoked. The other side of the coin is withdrawal. Both Moons like to run and hide when their emotions start to rage.

The other major influence of the Scorpio Moon is its increased influence toward lustful behavior. If you manage to stay free of depression, you may discover a sexual urge that needs some attention.

Cancer Moon Personality in the Sagittarius Moon

The warm influence of this Fire Moon can be very comforting. An attachment to the storybook romance is just one phase of the idealistic lifestyle nurtured by the Sagittarius Moon. Keep your intuition working as you make your choices. At times, the Sagittarius Moon will blind you to the realities of life.

Charlie, an immensely talented body-worker, has intuitive hands—he finds just the right spot without discussion. His natural, intuitive abilities are enhanced by his Cancer Moon. Once, while I received a massage, we talked about his clients over the course of a Sagittarius Moon. His clients had consistently commented on his gentle playfulness, and displayed their satisfaction with generous tips.

You may feel more personable in this Moon. Sagittarius' fiery energy adds fuel to your emotions, but does not strengthen their movement. It intensifies your feelings without pushing you toward further emotional extremes. It also intensifies peaceful, harmonious states of mind, which leads to a greater ability to fend off negative opinions.

This Sagittarius Moon will bring welcome relief from the Scorpio Moon. A positive outlook on life and a warm heart can take you a long way in this world. Guard against extended flights of fantasy and this stable Moon will greet you with a smile for the next two days.

Cancer Moon Personality in the Capricorn Moon

The last of the Earth Moons will complement your feelings of home and hearth, but its grounded, insensitive, and unemotional nature might be foreign to you.

In a way, it might be enjoyable to be unemotional for a short period of time. It is possible that the only effect this Capricorn Moon will have is to lessen your emotional swings, and to make them more manageable.

This would certainly be a good opportunity to work on your most taxing solo projects, especially those in which you have a vested interest. Make your financial decisions today if you want to adopt a cold, calculating point of view. Joe, a religious studies professor, uses this Moon to complete his tax return. This Moon will not turn you into a heartless person. It will just give you access to material ambitions if you need them.

Cancer Moon Personality in the Aquarius Moon

When it comes to mood swings, this Moon is certainly in its element. The Aquarius Moon will not affect the depth of emotions that you experience, but will influence you to change your mood on a whim. Even the Cancer Moon personality has not experienced the unpredictable mood swings that this Aquarius Moon will offer. The energetic influences you will receive from this Air Moon will be eclectic, to say the least.

The Aquarius Moon's energy is idealistic, but it tempts you to hide the emotions that come to the surface. Your quickly changing emotional state is apt to shift from elation to depression. When an Aquarius Moon takes an emotional dive, it happens very quickly. The cooling process can take just a couple of minutes.

You will be drawn to the energy of this Moon. If all goes well, it could be a very nice experience. Try to stay away from negative people and circumstances, because these are the biggest contributors to your mood changes.

Cancer Moon Personality in the Pisces Moon

Although a Water Moon transit is always an emotionally unpredictable time, this one has the potential for peace, enjoyment, and romance. The energies you will receive from this Moon are very similar to the natal energies from your Cancer Moon. They also differ enough for the two energies to marry nicely.

Optimism and a positive attitude offer substantial benefits. The only danger lies in the overt or implied opinions of others. Otherwise, you should have a great couple of days.

Romance will be in full swing. This Moon is a very romantic one, and romance is no stranger to you, either. Make some plans; go someplace with your significant other. Take advantage of these influences as you would good weather. Get outside and play a little in the sunshine. It's not often you have such an opportunity for fun and frolic. After an intense week of inner work and emotional stimulation at a rebirthing seminar, Ariel rewarded herself with skiing under the Pisces Moon.

Leo Moon

Your Lunar Profile

"Creative," "dramatic," and "proud" are but a few words used to describe your natal characteristics. Leo is a Masculine, Fire sign and will impart affection, generosity, and a need for control.

Pride is of importance to the Leo Moon personality. Like a lion, you are proud of your accomplishments and justifiably roar about your deeds. You like to be admired, but will seldom deign to ask for attention. Out-and-out bragging is more your style. You are flamboyant and like the center stage. Flattery is one way into your heart, but if you display a need for it, you may appear to be self-centered and egotistical. You are outgoing and dynamic with a flair for the dramatic.

These are qualities others admire in you, and these traits display your other attitudes and attributes in a very positive way. You have the energy to get things done, especially when motivated by your pride or need for recognition or glamour.

You are wonderfully romantic when your heart is comfortably connected to another. Being in love is very important. Your emotional integrity manifests in affectionate generosity.

Leo's fiery energy mixed with the Moon's creates emotionally heated passion. Your stardom shines in everything you do; you are comfortable with your emotions running free. In fact, suppressing your emotions is not easy for you and, if accomplished, will not last long.

Your dramatizations are fun, though never out of your control. Your need to be admired and recognized will lead you to describe your moods in extremes such as "bright as a supernova" or "apocalyptic." If negatively influenced, you might exaggerate so excessively that the actual circumstances become unrecognizable. Instead of nursing a cold in bed for two days, you may relate your near-death experience.

Jackie, my friend's oldest daughter, has a Leo Moon and is prone to extremes. She describes her life in tens and ones; she is never just "okay." Jackie is an optimist who exudes happiness and control. When asked about her life, Jackie will say that it is "wonderful," or "hellish."

When the positive aspects of your personality are not working for you, emotional gratification will come from being pushy and controlling. Pretentiousness and competitiveness are other negative ways of meeting your needs. The heated nature of the Leo Moon will get you through the downtime quickly. Release your emotions with dramatic intensity and you will be back on track in no time.

Living fast and loose is your style. Balance between your inner-self and your outer persona are essential. You can be very aware of your feelings and sensitive to the feelings of others. By developing a better understanding of your inner-self, you will be less inclined to rely on the emotional support of others and much more capable of being emotionally self-supporting. You may also find that by allowing others to see the true emotional you, they will respond in kind. You are very warm and caring. Full participation in life puts you in the fast lane, and offers all the rewards you seek.

Influences on the Leo Moon Personality

Leo Moon Personality in the Aries Moon

The fiery influences in this Moon will set off similar characteristics in your natal Moon. Pride can be a problem if taken too far. Pride in your accomplishments is one thing, demanding that others recognize your deeds is another. Your determination will also be displayed.

Along with this determination will come impatience and dominance. You will want things done your way. Try to de-intensify these feelings and you will be successful in getting along with others.

One benefit of this Moon is charm. When you are happy, others will share your happiness. A few kind words and a smile will instantly improve most situations. The intensity of this Fire Moon could add a large dose of flirtatiousness to your charming personality. Just remember that a little flirting goes a long way, and that excessive flirting causes trouble.

After a few drinks had loosened her inhibitions, Naomi, a Leo Moon personality, began a campaign of intense flirting with two men in a nightclub. When the first didn't immediately respond to her flirting, Naomi thought that he was uninterested, and she moved on to the second. As soon as she did, the first bought her a drink. Naomi decided to go home alone after her flirtation with the two men ended in a fight between them.

Leo Moon Personality in the Taurus Moon

This well-grounded Moon will have a subduing effect on your life as a whole. The sign of Taurus will influence you to slow down and relax. It has shown that it, too, can be of service in your life when a degree of steadfastness is required. Stubbornness is another byproduct of this Moon.

Typically, you can expect to be lethargic in a Taurus Moon. Both the Bull and the Lion are lazy by nature, and when these natural energies are combined, the result is the need for a nap. You may feel as though some things require too much effort or are not the priority they used to be. Unless this is a huge problem, relax. These feelings will pass soon enough. Besides, you could probably use a break.

Both the Bull and the Lion are also somewhat stubborn, and, when necessary, driven. You will be able to overcome the dulling effects of this Moon if you deem it important enough. Draw on the power of Leo—a little Fire will set you free.

Leo Moon Personality in the Gemini Moon

You may need to deal with an array of situations simultaneously under this two-faced Air Moon. As symbolized by the Twins, the Gemini Moon represents a division within your personality. Your skill with people will work well for you, but you will be unfocused and less attentive than usual.

Your mind will race but your thoughts may be disjointed. The Gemini Moon exhibits a good deal of intelligence, but the mind shifts from one subject to another so readily that no serious work can occur.

Your curiosity about the lives of others will prompt you to ask questions in order to delve into their deepest thoughts and desires. Reciprocity is difficult for you. It is easy to show your ego-based, outer personality. In this Moon you talk to everyone; however, displaying your inner-self to others, even to yourself, is a major undertaking. Should you choose to open up, you must be totally focused on letting your true self see the light of day; otherwise it won't happen.

In the Gemini Moon, you have the makings of a great host. Maybe it's time to have some friends over for drinks and dinner. Entertain them with your skill at any game requiring mental agility, and they will admire you.

Leo Moon Personality in the Cancer Moon

The watery influences of this Moon will extinguish your fiery traits of drive and flamboyance. In other ways, Fire and Water will mix, producing a steamy passionate heat. Sensitivity and passion will be enhanced in your relationships.

Jaime became unusually attentive to his wife's needs in this Moon—so much so that Karen jokes he is trying to compensate for a month of self-centeredness in a few days. Of course, the actual situation is not so extreme, but the Leo Moon personality exhibits itself primarily at the ends of the spectrum.

The increase in sensitivity with others will also be reflected in your relationship with yourself. It is time to look inward and get to know yourself better. Be aware of your needs and gently meet them. Reward yourself for a job well done.

Leo Moon Personality in the Leo Moon

You are at home in this energy. The Leo Moon will intensify the positive and negative components of your basic emotional structure.

You will be more prideful, and will be eager to talk about your deeds and dreams. Bragging can become an art form in this Moon. Dramatization and embellishment should be moderated. People will stop listening to and trusting you. The truth can only be stretched so far before it's no longer the truth.

You are a very loving individual, especially under the influence of the Leo Moon. Despite your generosity, you expect to be greatly appreciated. If this does not happen, beware of your disappointment turning to anger or stubbornness. Give the "gift of confidence" to a friend by admiring his or her special qualities.

Your warm, loving self will shine in this Moon. Show that inner-self to others without expectation. It will be easy to give, but more difficult to not demand reciprocation.

Leo Moon Personality in the Virgo Moon

This Earth Moon is famous for its analytical approach to life—it is logical and unemotional. This strategy for understanding others doesn't work well for you. Your emotions play a big role in your perceptions, and you don't appreciate others categorizing you.

This Moon will add confusion and frustration to your thought processes. You will feel the need to take a closer look at things before making decisions. You are accustomed to making decisions based on emotional criteria. Analysis is unimportant because you know what you want. The need to analyze drives you crazy.

Virgo is also a grounding Earth Moon. This could dampen your flamboyance, and make you seem a little withdrawn. Your normal, fiery energy level may also be reduced. This will help you focus on yourself.

Leo Moon Personality in the Libra Moon

The next couple of days could bring peace and harmony if you can stay emotionally available and are willing to accept your faults. This will be hard because it may be an affront to your pride, but can lead to much happiness.

Romance is in the air surrounding this Moon. When you are open to your own emotions, you also allow others to see the kind, caring, loving person you really are under all of that flash and pizazz. Honesty with others could develop quickly into romance. Honesty is the path to openness, and intimacy is the result.

Your attraction to the more luxurious things in life is enhanced in this Moon. You may find yourself indulging in more elegant comforts than you would generally allow yourself.

Have some fun during this very comfortable Moon. You will have trouble making choices, but that won't interfere with your enjoyment of the next few days.

Leo Moon Personality in the Scorpio Moon

"Intense" is the best word to describe the Scorpio Moon. The time has come for your emotions to go into overdrive. This Moon will add some secrecy to your lifestyle but will also add the desire for others to share all. Jealousy will erupt when this dichotomy does not work out as you wish.

The Scorpio Moon facilitates intuition. You can receive much information through your intuition as long as you remain open to it. This will require honesty with yourself and a willingness to share your emotional responses with others. Since this Moon will help you to be more secretive, you may not be willing to open yourself, leaving the opportunity to misinterpret your "feelings." Your intuition will still receive messages but the conscious mind may not understand them. Jealousy may raise its ugly head based on your perceptions of things you don't understand.

On the positive side, the passionate intensity of this Moon can certainly increase a person's sex drive. The answering machine at my friends' house had the following message, "Hi, this is Karen, and Jaime (in their separate voices). It's a Scorpio Moon and we're busy. Leave a message."

Leo Moon Personality in the Sagittarius Moon

Laugh at yourself and others will laugh with you. The fiery nature of Sagittarius will blend well with your own burning energy to create the opportunity for a very good time.

The Sagittarius Moon does deal with the inner-self. This is a good time to examine your emotional responses to recent and past predicaments, and to understand what you did and how you felt about it. Share the results of your introspection. Laughter may ensue if you take a humorous look at yourself—others may chime in with their own stories. Your need to be at center stage will be met, and your flamboyance will add to the fun.

The positive aspects of life will shine during this Moon. The negative aspects are always there, but it will be harder to find them. Keep smiling. The positive energy you are feeling will permeate into everything you do. Your sexual attraction to another will be more intensely playful if you are with the right person.

Leo Moon Personality in the Capricorn Moon

This Moon will demand that you pay attention to the material world at hand. Practicality and earthy realism are the means by which this Moon conducts its business. Flamboyance has no place in this Moon. It's time to begin detail-oriented work. This could be a great opportunity to do your taxes or balance your checkbook.

This Moon will not be conducive to planning, dreaming, or working on your long-term goals. All of that stuff will seem like fantasy and you won't be in the mood to deal with fantasies. This Moon will bring you down to earth.

You may become phlegmatic if your are not interested in productive materialism or in detailed work. Energy levels will be low and the desire to respond will be even lower. Goals in which you have a personal stake are the best motivators in this Moon. Focus on tangible goals, and remember to keep them practical and achievable with hard work.

A dear friend, Naomi, mentioned that she felt grounded and lacked the energy to make sales calls, and that these feelings were becoming cyclical. I suggested that the Capricorn Moon was at play and she might consider spending the day in the office in this Moon rather than committing to a full day of customers. Naomi now takes advantage of the grounded Capricorn Moon by working on her monthly sales and commission reports.

Leo Moon Personality in the Aquarius Moon

This Moon is the opposite of your natal Moon, so in some ways you may feel attracted to Aquarian influences. You will be easily influenced to rely on your flashy and ostentatious personality rather than dealing with your emotions. Your time would be better spent attempting to experience the deep feelings of this Moon. An honest effort here might yield significant rewards.

This Air Moon is known for its ability to ignore the emotional responses that arise in life. Instead of dealing with and learning from them, the Aquarius Moon persona will store emotions in an inner reservoir and hope the dam never breaks.

The response you receive from other people will be one of respect and admiration. To them, you are a justifiably proud individual, who achieves success in life and accomplishes goals. You go your own way; you listen to the advice of others but almost never accept it. Emotional integrity will breed self-admiration as well.

Leo Moon Personality in the Pisces Moon

It will feel wonderful to slide for a few days, especially if it's been a hard month and the energy-conserving Lion needs a break. You can learn a lot about emotions in the Pisces Moon, or you can just relax and be yourself.

You will have no trouble in getting exactly what you want during this Moon, at least in the emotional arena. Pisces Moon energy does not have the strength to stand up to the fiery intensity of the Leo Moon. Romantic influences abound. Your Leo personality eclipses the Pisces Moon in many ways, but this romantic Moon will still be felt. Unlike some Moon signs that rock your world, the Pisces Moon will be warm and gentle.

This Moon can be very beneficial. You can selectively accept the emotional input that your inner-self offers. Take this opportunity to single out some of your past issues and allow them to be scrutinized in a safe manner.

Virgo Moon

Your Lunar Profile

Virgo is the sixth sign of the Zodiac. It is ruled by the planet Mercury, who in Roman mythology is the winged messenger of the gods. Virgo is a Feminine, Earth sign. With your Moon in this sign you will be practical and hardworking, but will not be dedicated to the idea of working hard for its own sake. You will easily motivate yourself to work hard toward a particular end or goal. You can be exacting and detailed, intellectual pursuits are a passion, and a good sense of logic is your resource. This combination of precision and intellect is well suited for problem solving and analysis. It is not unusual for you to analyze all you read. The Virgo Moon personality is critical; you love to analyze and express your views.

People with a Virgo Moon will often be involved politics and in their communities on local and national levels. This is due in part to their critical nature and in part because they are very caring. You will devote yourself to a service-related organization and to the people you most care about.

It is important that you learn to listen to your inner-self. This is an area in which you might be reluctant to work, but when developed could yield fantastic results. You have the innate ability to see through delusions. In order to do this, you must trust your inner voice, even though this can be very difficult for you. Instinctively you hear this inner voice but often choose to ignore it. Your latent psychic abilities will emerge if you listen to and trust yourself. With these tools at your disposal, you will be very perceptive and sensitive to the people and situations around you. Self-confidence will be your attribute rather than a deficiency.

Your tendency is to seek stability and to be self-sacrificing in relationships. Exciting, spontaneous romantic interludes are not your specialty, but occur when you understand and listen to your heart. You look for security when dealing with others, especially in your love life, because in the emotional realm you are very practical and well grounded. This does not mean passion is beyond you—you are a passionate person when trusting your instincts.

The downside to the Virgo Moon is that you can become obsessive and analytical; Virgo is known for perfectionism. This will lead to self-doubt because your work will never be good enough, and, therefore, never complete. You also have the ability to worry incessantly. When you are not in touch with your innermost feelings, you buy into self-created delusions. Your salvation comes from your inherent powers of discrimination, which is all the more reason to trust your instincts and enjoy life.

You can become obsessive about health and exercise, and you may analyze your exercise program and diet to excess. You like to look good, and only think you look good when you feel good. Consequently, the best balance for you is to eat well and exercise moderately. Your self-image is one of a fit and healthy person. You can use this image to be positive and productive.

Influences on the Virgo Moon Personality

Virgo Moon Personality in an Aries Moon

The Aries Moon will provide you with some rather intense energy. You may find this energy distasteful as your level of patience diminishes. In addition to your normally exacting nature, you will have a tendency to become assertive and to appear insensitive to those around you.

The "fire in your belly" will be of benefit to you with proper preparation. This is a time to get things done. When details would only slow you down, the "hurry up and get it done" attitude of this Moon will push you to completion. Any project that requires attention to detail during this Moon will need an extra measure of patience, because it will be difficult to contain the erratic Aries energy. A former coworker, Michelle, is amazingly productive in the Aries Moon. She chooses to complete projects which require action rather than analysis.

Virgo Moon Personality in a Taurus Moon

This should be a fairly comfortable sign for you. Taurus is a solid Earth sign that will complement the well-grounded Virgo Moon. You will be a more practical than usual and focus on the basics. Your energy level will be up and your mood good. It will be more difficult for others to raise your blood pressure during this Moon; however, a lustful, even carnal side of you could sneak out rather unexpectedly. The Taurus Moon is rather seductive and is fairly overt about it. You may find yourself embarrassed by your directness in conversations. This Moon will be conducive to just about any task put before you, including physical relationships.

Virgo Moon Personality in a Gemini Moon

The Gemini Moon will provide the proper energy level for conquering intellectual pursuits. Your detail-oriented intellect will be aroused in the Gemini Moon. The flighty influences of this Air Moon will expand your intellectual boundaries. Take an innovative look at your life and the things troubling you. Try a new approach in dealing with an old problem. It's easier to cross self-imposed boundaries. Be unreasonable in your approach to possible solutions. In other words, consider solutions or ideas that do not appear to be reasonable. Often, an apparently unreasonable solution holds the most creative promise.

The downside of this Moon is the possibility of becoming excessively creative, to the point of losing your focus or forgetting your original intent. This is exemplified by conversations in which examples or metaphors are used to make a point, but you get so caught in them that you forget the point you intended to make. Joyce, my son's kindergarten teacher, used a traffic sign as a metaphor to further emphasize her point in one of our conversations. In her next sentence, she used another traffic sign analogy, and then another, and another. Joyce quickly listed traffic sign after traffic sign as her desired point faded into a metaphoric litany, "slippery when wet, dangerous curves, reduce speed ahead, no stopping or standing . . . ."

Virgo Moon Personality in a Cancer Moon

The Cancer Moon will tug on your heartstrings and highlight a need for security. Your moods could change quickly and without much provocation. You may begin to feel that the details in your life are overwhelming, and may not see the forest for the trees.

Troy, who has a natal Virgo Moon, wanted to talk after an emotionally intense night. His swollen face and puffy eyes said more than words. Troy realized that he had been lying to himself about issues of integrity. His fears were running his life, and this realization was very difficult for Troy to swallow. My only advice to Troy was to fasten his seat belt and stay open to all truths. The coldness that gripped his heart would fade as he accepted the truth—he was not less of a person for acknowledging his fears, and these admissions would bolster his integrity.

Cancer Moons have the ability to strip away the defenses that the ego uses to keep up outer images. Be prepared to deal with yourself honestly. If you try to fool yourself, you will wind up at odds with yourself; your inner-self will disrupt your usually well-grounded demeanor with an emotional outburst. Examine that which is truly important to you. Introspection is most easily accomplished during this Moon. Your defenses will be down, and others can easily hurt your feelings since you will be more susceptible to criticism.

Virgo Moon Personality in a Leo Moon

Fire energy will bring welcome relief from the Cancer Moon. The Leo Moon provides frolicsome energy—be frisky and approach life with zeal.

You may feel as though you are a cut above the rest and deserve recognition. If this is the case, recognize yourself with a reward such as dinner at a restaurant or a movie. It's best not to depend on others to fulfill your needs. You will be the tiniest bit hyperactive and the lack of recognition could undermine your enjoyment of the situation.

If you must work during this Moon, try to tackle a project that gives you gratification and satisfaction. Troy returned a few days after his Cancer Moon transit and reported that his emotional world had calmed and was transformed. He became extremely productive, tied up a number of loose ends, and proudly advertised his many accomplishments.

Virgo Moon Personality in a Virgo Moon

This will feel like coming home. You are comfortable with the Virgo Moon's familiar energy. Your basic traits are fed in this Moon. The grounded nature of an Earth Moon, like this one, will almost always make you feel better about your circumstances.

However, as it is in your nature to be discriminating, you could find yourself in deep analysis, weighing a situation's positive and negative attributes. Extreme analytical behavior could seem detrimental at first glance, but it could be put to very good use solving that multifaceted problem from which even your detailed mind had backed away. Your basic lunar traits will be magnified by the Virgo Moon. This intensity may cause you to be argumentative, or to take either side of an argument, which, with your intellect, you are certainly capable of doing. This is a time to revel in who you are, and to recognize the traits you really like best about yourself.

I have learned to avoid games of strategy with one of my friends, who has both a Virgo Moon and a Virgo Sun. When he's feeling particularly analytical, I'm routinely trounced by his detailed intellect.

Virgo Moon Personality in a Libra Moon

Indecisiveness will be the norm during this Moon. The Libra Moon is not known for decisiveness; however, it is very capable of revealing choices hidden from view. It is common to be unable to make the simplest choices. When asked in a polite greeting how he was feeling during a Libra Moon a friend replied, "I can't decide." It is best to plan to work on repetitive tasks that you've done before and require no decisions in order to complete during this Moon. Be more outrageous, even lavish, if you are so inclined.

The airy Libra Moon will bring out your need for companionship. You may want to spend time with friends. This is a good Moon for a party. You are very sociable and will especially crave the companionship of the opposite sex.

Virgo Moon Personality in a Scorpio Moon

Your fuse could be short if others meddle in your affairs. The Scorpio Moon will bring secrecy to your life. If you need to take care of private matters, this is a wonderful time to do so. This Water Moon will raise the intensity of your emotions. In a Scorpio Moon the increased intensity will occur primarily with others' perception of you. The level of trust you place in others will be in question for the next few days. In this Moon, you like to be admired more than usual, but will keep your plans to yourself.

A Virgo Moon acquaintance spoke incessantly about sex and offered graphic details in the Scorpio Moon; however, when asked questions about her statements, she claimed that they were inappropriate and refused to answer them. The boundary between conversation and interrogation was not clearly defined—intimacy was not a problem when she initiated the dialogue, but she had difficulty in accepting it from others.

Your need for emotional intensity and admiration may be expressed through sex. The Scorpio Moon is notorious for heightening the sex drive and magnifying the need for passion. This is a great time to spend in the company of a partner with whom you share a passionate, intimate relationship.

Virgo Moon Personality in a Sagittarius Moon

The fiery energy of Sagittarius is going to make you more outgoing. Back off and have a little fun. The best course of action in this Moon is to be spontaneous and enjoy yourself. Moving and adapting to life's changes will be easy; however, you may be suspicious of others' motives. By taking the pressure off yourself, you will find it easier to deal with others, even in the face of these suspicions.

I was once simultaneously involved with three Virgo Moon personalities: my boss, a coworker, and a girlfriend. Even though they had uniquely different personalities, their emotional responses held many similarities. For instance, during a Sagittarius Moon, they invariably would be upbeat, fun-loving, and optimistic.

In this Moon you will be generally optimistic and could easily become motivated to take on a big project that you have been resisting. If you should make a commitment, use this time to work on the overall plan and to have fun with it. Detailed analysis during this Moon will not work out well. Be sure to save time for enjoyable activities.

Virgo Moon Personality in a Capricorn Moon

"Practical" and "productive" are the two words that best describe the Capricorn Moon's influences. This Moon will make you less detail-oriented and increase your level of success. Hard work will be a joy as long it's practical.

Since you are well grounded in this Earth Moon, you will be highly resistant to emotional upsets. When they do occur, you will be intensely affected. You will become increasingly private, even withdrawn. Avoid emotional disconnection from yourself and others.

In the Capricorn Moon you are happiest when dealing with your possessions and money in the material world. It will probably not feel right to share these resources with others.

Virgo Moon Personality in an Aquarius Moon

The Aquarius Moon is an Air Moon of a different sort. In this Moon you will feel separated from life and from others. You may not really care what happens, except to you. Your emotions will run very deep, but you will not share them with others.

You may appear to be calm and cool-headed with little or no emotional volatility. This is not a time for introspection, but for separation. The Aquarius Moon is usually an uncomfortable place for you unless life has been hectic and you need some time alone. Take care of yourself and don't expect too much. There is a greater potential for trouble in this Moon than there is success.

Virgo Moon Personality in a Pisces Moon

Your psychic and intuitive abilities will be enhanced in this Water Moon. Increased attunement to the emotional states of others make you more caring and nurturing. A heartfelt need to help will arise from your sensitivity. Your love relationships will stabilize and flourish, creating opportunities for romance.

Just as you are more caring during this Moon, you will expect others to be more caring and sensitive towards you. Your feelings may be hurt because this may not always happen. You will be more susceptible to manipulation. Use your intuitive abilities to better understand others' desires. Your logical approach to life is still in place, but you should make your decisions based on both logic and intuition.

The sign of Pisces is the opposite of Virgo in the Zodiac. These opposing influences affect your physical health. During the Pisces Moon, you may feel ill or under the weather without medical reason, perhaps to the point of hypochondria. Listen closely to your body and avoid supposition.

Libra Moon

Your Lunar Profile

Libra is the seventh sign in the Zodiac. It is a Masculine, Air sign, which is ruled by Venus, the goddess of love. This sign is a curious combination of qualities—it has Masculine influences and is ruled by the Feminine. This one statement sums up the way you deal with your inner-self. The feminine aspects that control your relationships make you among the most loving and caring individuals of all twelve signs. You are charming and diplomatic, romantic and cheerful. Marriage, family, and relationships are of great importance. You become intensely concerned when peace and harmony are not maintained. You have an eye for beauty and will instinctively search for it.

The masculine aspects of this sign are your well-honed instinct for self-preservation and a reluctantly tough inner-self. Consideration of others' feelings works better for you than a hard-as-steel approach; however, you can be as tough as needed. You are often underestimated because your feminine qualities make you appear to be weak, but a would-be opponent quickly discovers his or her error.

The Libra Moon makes you indecisive, especially when it come to trivialities, such as your dinner selection. In conversation, you jump from one subject to another, leaving others in a trail of dust. Your thought processes are quick, but you sometimes try to solve a bigger problem than actually exists.

You are a good partner, but this can also be your downfall. When negatively influenced by the Libra Moon, you become dependent on your companion. It's difficult to balance self-reliance with companionship. Because of your innate need to be with others, you can feel less than adequate when you are not in a relationship. Insecurity can lead to the manipulation of others to gain their acceptance, approval, and love. The need for approval and acceptance of others also makes you very susceptible to manipulation. You will often buy into an idea or action without fully understanding all of its facets or even trying to do so. If it's important to someone you care about, it must be of importance to you.

The ability to maintain good personal and public relations is one of your greatest strengths. You are well liked by others because you treat them with respect. You believe in the adage, "Treat others the way you wish to be treated."

The Libra Moon is represented by the Scales, which should always be in balance. You become very frustrated when some form of injustice tips the scales, especially when it doesn't tip in your favor. You don't like to be judged negatively, particularly when a close friend or lover makes these judgments.

I have a Libra Moon and hold fairness as a high ideal. Justice is important to me. The tarot card, Justice, visually describes my attitude toward fairness. It portrays a man of wisdom sitting on a throne holding a set of perfectly balanced scales in one hand and a sword in the other. The wise judge on the throne keeps the law. The rules in his realm are fair and equally pervasive. When the scales of justice tilt out of balance, he doles out punishment. I respect this message. The further out of balance the scales become, the less I like it.

You are innately loving and romantic; these are your tools for acquiring emotional security. It's important to learn that you must be secure within yourself before you can be secure in a relationship. When you are inwardly happy, you will be wholly fulfilled.

Influences on the Libra Moon Personality

Libra Moon Personality in the Aries Moon

This Fire Moon will add intensity to any emotional experience. Aries likes things to move along—it won't tolerate sitting and waiting for opportunities to present themselves. The Aries Moon transit is both positively and negatively aspected.

The Aries Moon will provide enough influence to force you to make a decision and to take action. Whatever your choices may be, you will make them, prioritize them, and begin. It is very likely that you will choose the things you like the least to be among the first to get done. It's even possible to juggle several activities at once, such as like laundry, housecleaning, and cooking breakfast.

The other side of the Aries Moon is impatience. Waiting will be your least favorite activity, and waiting on someone else will be an irritation. Communication is especially volatile. You will expect your point of view to be understood immediately. If not, your impatience will turn to frustration or anger. Patience is essential if you are going to get along with others.

I'm usually accepting of others, and give them plenty of space to be themselves. In the Aries Moon, I find myself quick to lose my temper. My patience is at its monthly low. I'm usually argumentative and can become angry with less provocation. Consequently, I have found that emphasizing excitement and adventure works better than tackling joint projects.

When presented with the opportunity to enjoy yourself, this too will be powered by the Aries Moon. There is always room for more fun as long as you don't have to wait.

Libra Moon Personality in the Taurus Moon

This strong Earth sign can give you the inner strength to accomplish or attain anything you desire. Love is in motion during this

Moon. You may find yourself moving a little slowly due to the grounding nature of this Moon, which does not tolerate your indecisiveness.

This Moon brings out your fortitude. You will be stubborn enough to demand the right of choice, and stubborn enough to not invoke this right until good and ready. This time could also be very productive in the earthly realms.

The Libra Moon has the ability to be lazy, and the well-grounded Taurus Moon can be a lazy Moon. This is good time to relax and play. Enjoy several of your favorite pastimes at once, since you will probably be unable to decide which one to do first.

My Sun sign is Taurus, so I find it easy in the Taurus Moon to put stress on hold and just have fun. A fun-loving companion will often help me to shift gears and enhance my playful nature.

Companionship is very desirable in this Moon. Both of these signs lean toward romance as they are ruled by the goddess of love. The Taurus Moon emphasizes sharing, which fits in very well with the Libra Moon's ideals. In the Taurus Moon your loving and caring nature will be further amplified, though you won't jump off a cliff for love in this Moon. Under this Earth sign, you will be more practical about getting to know the other person and will start a relationship slowly. Unlike the Aries Moon, Taurus has plenty of patience.

Libra Moon Personality in the Gemini Moon

The Gemini Moon, represented by the Twins, is an Air sign. This Moon is even more scattered than the Libra Moon.

Your communication skills will be honed to a razor-sharp edge. You like to talk and this Moon will intensify that desire. Gemini is also an intellectual sign; hopefully, it will keep others from labeling you an airhead, though the way you segue from topic to topic may give another impression.

People will listen to what you have to say, especially people of the opposite sex, because your natural charm is enhanced by this Moon. Be careful of flirtatious behavior—in this Moon you could easily give someone the wrong impression. I have done this many times in a Gemini Moon, and have learned to avoid flirtatious conversations altogether.

Your wit and intellect will be very quick. This is a fantastic opportunity for networking—try entertaining or making a few sales calls. Watch your mood, since your quick wit could quickly turn into sarcasm. This is a danger only around people who don't take you seriously.

Libra Moon Personality in the Cancer Moon

A Cancer Moon can be a wonderful experience if you are emotionally fit, secure, and stable. It will help you to see the areas of your inner-self that need improvement.

A day at the beach is one of the best ways to manage a Cancer Moon. A watery environment is a good catalyst for an honest, introspective look at yourself and your emotional fitness. Places like the beach, a lake, or near a river are great spots, but any place in nature will work just as well. I love the beach, especially in a Cancer Moon.

Be willing to open yourself up to truthful self-examination, but don't beat yourself up. Learn why you react the way you do. Knowledge is power, and the more you know about yourself, the more powerful you become. Don't forget to turn on that charm; it will even improve your disposition.

When you have your emotional life in order, a Cancer Moon is an enriching time. Readily accessible emotions open new possibilities. You may bond with others more easily, and your relationships will be more intimate. In fact, a day at a secluded beach with loved ones could be a great way to take advantage of this Moon.

I remember an evening when Ariel and I were driving back from a firewalk, enjoying a pleasant conversation. Our words suddenly became tense, and tears appeared out of nowhere. We worked through our feelings and banished the negative emotions which had surprised us. Afterwards, Ariel remarked that we must have been in a Cancer Moon. She was correct.

Libra Moon Personality in the Leo Moon

This Fire Moon will warm your emotions. Take gentle control of your surroundings and attract lots of attention doing it. Inner security will not be a problem with Leo's warm energy. Your everyday charm will be supplemented by the Leo Moon's warm character and laid-back attitude. You will be easier to talk to and more sincere.

As you assume leadership in your life, recognition is likely to come your way. Your decision-making ability will be enhanced as your emotional needs are met, thus clearing a place for the Lion's nobility to shine through. All of this recognition and noble acceptance will reflect in your own view of yourself. Emotional security will grow from accepting the reflection of your innerself as it really is, and not as you project it.

I always enjoy the warmth of the Leo Moon, especially after a difficult Cancer Moon. This Fire Moon dries the tears and warms the heart. There is enough energy available to get me moving again.

Libra Moon Personality in the Virgo Moon

This Moon can drive you crazy. You already lack the ability to make simple decisions and this analytical Moon drives you to further debate your decisions. Instead of just making a choice, now you will want to look at all the facts. This Moon will inspire you to analyze everything in your life which has not been firmly decided. It will also cause you to question your needs and desires.

Once, I went shopping for clothes in a Virgo Moon. My travel plans included a trip to South America. I wanted some sturdy, light clothes that would work well in the jungle and mountaintops. The assistance of the salesperson in that department was not enough to satisfy my need for analysis. Before I was done, I spoke with two other salespeople from different parts of the store. I examined every stitch of a new high-tech fabric and decided that the zipper didn't look sturdy enough. After leaving the store to "sleep on it," I went to another store and asked the same questions, in search of the one all-important detail, convinced there was more to learn about pants. I still didn't make a purchase, and opted to wait for the spring line that was due to be out a few weeks later.

Most people will agree that it is a good idea to check all the facts in order to make an informed choice, but this can be taken to extremes. After all, how many people do you know who ask for the factory test reports on a new car before they purchase it? This is especially true of a Libra Moon personality. You have enough of a struggle deciding on the color much less deciding if twenty foot-pounds is an adequate torque specification. Relax during this Moon, lie in the grass, and analyze the clouds.

Libra Moon Personality in the Libra Moon

You will feel comfortable here because it's the home of your Moon; however, comfort is not always a good thing. Comfort comes from recognizing yourself, and you may not be happy with what you see in the mirror. If so, this place may feel unhappily familiar.

All of your emotional qualities will be enhanced in this Moon. Use this time to look at yourself. Are these the emotional qualities that make you happy? Looking in the mirror is not always easy, but if you take a good look you will see the truth. The person looking back at you is your best friend.

You treat everyone you meet with courtesy, respect, and kindness. You are warm and loving in your circle of friends. If you want to be treated similarly, you must treat yourself like a best friend. Once you have developed a rapport yourself, others will see your true qualities.

It is easy to break your concentration and lose track of what you are doing under the Libra Moon's influence. Due to my absent-mindedness and lack of focus in this Moon, I have been called an air head for good reason. I have left my apartment and returned to retrieve forgotten items four to five times before remembering everything. I have missed exits and forgotten the purpose of my trip halfway to my destination. Sometimes I have dialed a phone number only to forget who I'm calling when the phone is answered.

Libra Moon Personality in the Scorpio Moon

"Sexually intense" could be the motto of this Water Moon. The influences of this Moon are simple—intensity of emotions with an emphasis on the physical world.

The Scorpio Moon is more than just a sexual influence. This Water Moon will affect your emotions in many ways, but it specializes in carnal desires. As long as you allow yourself to experience emotional changes, this Moon will primarily drive your sexual desires. This can, at times, be more intense than you care for, but if you stay open to it, you will rediscover your sensuality. The Scorpio Moon's influence has exposed me to more physical desires than I care to remember. There have been many moments of great enjoyment, but there have also been times I would rather forget.

There is a good deal of romantic energy tucked away in all of this intensity. You may find you are more comfortable in this romantic atmosphere than you might otherwise be. This sounds unusual as you are a romantic at heart, but if you allow these feelings to do their work, you will respond to romance with sensuality.

Libra Moon Personality in the Sagittarius Moon

Your innate charm will be magnified by this Fire Moon. Sagittarius doesn't have a lazy aspect but it does encourage a relaxed environment. This is the perfect Moon to follow Scorpio, which caused those intense sensual and romantic feelings to start bubbling. The Sagittarius Moon takes the next step by creating a space for warm friendship and relaxed, playful interaction.

Take an unstructured approach to life. Let your energies run in the direction they choose and make the most of the journey. In this Moon you won't be intensely emotional. This is more like an active vacation. Your buttons will be harder to find, so others will not push them as often. The only trouble that may arise is in respecting boundaries within relationships. You may be tempted to stray from commitments, and if you cross those boundaries, you will feel carefree now and guilty later.

Be happy with yourself and accept your emotions. The inner you needs time to play and relax. Give yourself time and the rewards will be evident in your attitude. Watch how your feelings change as your outlook towards life changes—there is always something to learn.

Libra Moon Personality in the Capricorn Moon

This Earth Moon will focus on security. The focus won't be on the security of your house and possessions, but the inner peace and emotional security that comes from a healthy home and lifestyle. This is a practical Moon, and in it you will work hard to achieve what is most important to you. These achievements can vary in scope but usually come from the same root: emotional security and stability.

In this Moon, I invariably look at my goals and how my financial situation fits into the plan. If I've put off balancing my checkbook, it gets done in the Capricorn Moon. My practicality quotient is very high and I'm able to let go of many things in this Moon that I would hold on to in another Moon.

You may feel protective of your home space, your financial status, and the well-being of your family and yourself. This need for protection is just another offshoot of the emotional security issue. Work on making your life more secure, and do this by first becoming more secure with your own emotions.

You are a sensitive person and this Moon is known for suppressing feelings. Don't let this get in your way. Examine your need for emotional security. Is it warranted or based in fear? If fear is the dominant force, release it.

Libra Moon Personality in the Aquarius Moon

Feelings in this Moon will be difficult to access. The Aquarius Moon will increase your mental activity. You will be less likely to discuss everything with everybody, or to jump from one topic to another, but will certainly be able to hold your own in any conversation. Your charm works well for you, but you may hide your emotions behind that charm.

The Aquarius Moon will not encourage you to open yourself to anyone. What is inside is best left inside and out of reach. In fact, you won't appreciate others' efforts to be close. This may create a conflict between your need for intimacy and the Aquarian need for emotional detachment. There could be moments in which secrecy makes sense as your powers of decision will not be enhanced at all in this Moon. If others are dealing with you in a less-than-open manner, you may be inclined to do the same. If you associate with close friends during this Moon, you will be able to better focus on your needs and still have a good time with the gang.

The Aquarius Moon tends to be dull for me. Since it instills a need to hide my emotions from the world, I find it more difficult to really get involved and to be committed. Sometimes I feel down, but I usually opt for light conversation and friendly exchanges. I save the real work for an Earth Moon.

Libra Moon Personality in the Pisces Moon

This Water sign is truly romantic. The sexual intensity of the Scorpio Moon has passed and the sensitive, sensual, romantic has arrived to work his or her magic. Focus on your primary relationship. With your charm and elegance, you will sweep your partner right off their feet.

Use your intuitive powers. If you are not in a committed relationship, you could easily be caught up in the idea of a storybook romance and lose sight of reality. Your intuition, if you listen to it, will help you to stay grounded and not run off to Las Vegas for a spontaneous, midnight wedding ceremony.

Enjoy your feelings of love and harmony. There is no better time. Happiness can be found in the arms of your mate if you will trust your feelings and let them see the real you. I'm a hopeless romantic and this suits me just fine.

Scorpio Moon

Your Lunar Profile

The eighth sign of the Zodiac, Scorpio, is a Water sign ruled by two planetary gods: Pluto, ruler of the underworld; and Mars, the god of war. It is a Feminine sign that has a close connection to the Moon and to emotions. This is a powerful Moon that is more intense than any other because of its planetary rulers. Pluto's underworld influence hides emotions. Mars is perpetually prepared for emotional battle. Combined, these two rulers influence you to be intense and secretive.

You are very intuitive and your emotions run very deep. So deep, in fact, that you can be very powerful and secretive. You can easily dominate another but also find it easy to withdraw to your inner world. "Passion" is the word that best describes you. You are passionate about all aspects of your life. It is hard for you to let anyone in because your passion can become excessive. Your memory is phenomenal, but then again, the inability to forget can be a mixed blessing.

When describing your personality, each trait should be preceded by the word "very" or "intensely." Your magnetic personality draws people to you, and you don't want for potential friends or companions in your life. Your Moon is a true seductress, and makes you quite alluring and undeniable.

With close ties to the Moon, you are incredibly intuitive. With very little effort, you can hone your instincts to the extent that you can never be fooled. The truth will not elude you, regardless of its nature. It's next to impossible for others to hide things from you and totally impossible to hide from yourself. Others can develop a distaste for your intuitive abilities, because they feel that you snoop too much. Avoid verbalizing your intuitively gained knowledge. Once you've harnessed self-discipline, your intuitive abilities combined with the strength of your inner-self will make you very powerful.

Your memory serves you very well. A photographic memory is a wonderful characteristic, except when it keeps you from forgiving. You may have trouble forgiving anyone that has ever treated you poorly, especially yourself. People do make mistakes, and if you hold them or yourself forever accountable, you will never be happy in life. Forgiveness is an admirable trait that is worth taking to extremes.

You have the ability to withdraw and to be lost in your own world for periods of time. No one is allowed to share your inner world, except perhaps your soul mate.

You are an intensely sensual person. If you understand and instinctively use your sensuality, you can be alluring without crossing the line. Your sensuality has a tremendous appetite. You want to feel connected with others—meeting your need for physical intimacy is important. If this does not happen, sex can become a crutch that is used to replace the affection you are missing.

If you harness the gifts you've received from your Scorpio Moon you can be powerful, alluring, intimate, and intimidating. The choice is yours.

Influences on the Scorpio Moon Personality

Scorpio Moon Personality in the Aries Moon

The fiery nature of this sign is attractive to you, since its planetary ruler is also Mars. The heat from this Moon blends well with your passionate outlook. It will not add intensity, but it will add drive and motivation.

This Moon will help you to get moving. It is a "take charge and get it done" Moon. The Aries-influenced persona does not like to just sit and play. It will push you to accomplish something. Use this time to make major strides toward your goals.

The Aries Moon is also known for its passion. Granted, its passion does not hold a candle to yours, but the energies will feel comfortable to you.

Your emotions may run hot in this Moon. A disagreement can quickly turn to anger. This is especially prevalent when your intuition tells you something different than what you hear from the other person. The trick is to know when you are intuitively obtaining the truth, and when your own emotions, such as jealousy, are clouding your judgment.

Scorpio Moon Personality in the Taurus Moon

Don't get buried by this Earth Moon. It's well grounded and could drain your energy. You might think that you need to rest after the Aries Moon, but as the days roll on, you will feel your energy continuing to slip away.

It is the nature of the Bull to be a homebody. You may find that cuddling on the couch in front of a warm fire just what you need. This can be a very sensual Moon if your relationship is firmly rooted. The Taurus Moon emphasizes a comfortable, safe home and an emotionally secure lifestyle. This is a good time to take a look at any issues you may have with security.

You will be very warm-hearted during this Moon. You may appear to be weak or drained, but if you are happy inside, all is well. Be yourself and enjoy the intimacy of the person closest to you.

Scorpio Moon Personality in the Gemini Moon

This Moon induces a complete lack of focus. The airy nature of this Moon will affect your perception of the intuitive information you receive. You may feel mentally scattered and not sure of your instincts. You use your intuitive abilities, whether you realize it or not, to guide you in most areas of your life. Your intuition is attuned to the truth, and helps to keep your passionate emotional responses in line with your desires. When the cosmic messages are being jammed, as they are in this Moon, you are less able to find your way and your emotions have more freedom to react.

You may become jealous where your primary relationship is concerned. This is also a flirtatious Moon. Flirting by your partner with another could send you over the edge. In order to offset the emotional responses centered around jealousy, you may become very possessive. If your mate can't leave your sight, there's reason to worry. Be careful with this Moon.

Scorpio Moon Personality in the Cancer Moon

Cancer is also a Water Moon, but unlike the Scorpio Moon it is very moody. You appreciate and are at home in this Moon's romantic energy, but you are not accustomed to moodiness, which certainly will be uncomfortable.

Your feelings run deep, and in the Cancer Moon you will be highly sensitive to others' feelings. It will also be easy for others to hurt your feelings. You will react more readily to stimulation from another, be it positive or negative.

Emotions will vary in intensity but more often than not will be on the upper end of the scale. This is due to the combination of your emotional intensity with this Moon's emotive influence.

Your best prescription for this Moon's influence is to try to stay calm, and to learn from your reactions.

Cancer Moons can be very difficult for the Scorpio Moon people I know. I regularly visit with my counselor friends and each time we meet or talk they ask when the Cancer Moon is coming. It affects them so much they have developed their own "cure."

Scorpio Moon Personality in the Leo Moon

This could be a beneficial Moon. The Leo Moon encourages strength, willfulness, and pride. The Fire energy provided by this Moon will highlight your warm heart, vivacious personality, and charm.

You exhibit the same basic traits as the person with a natal Leo Moon, except that these traits are of the inner-self rather than the outer-self. Emotionally you've a great deal of strength and willpower. You are full of life and love deeply.

When these two sets of lunar characteristics are combined, you will become wholly strong and willful, "a force to be reckoned with." Generally, you will be loving and caring, sensitive and strong, and fully able to overpower lesser wills with the strength of your constitution.

Consider using your willpower, strength, sensitivity, and charm to find a quiet beach and lie in the Sun for a few days. As one of my counselor friends noted, "I like to reward myself for a job well done."

Scorpio Moon Personality in the Virgo Moon

This is another well-grounded Earth Moon, but with a twist. The Virgo Moon inspires analysis of all things, including your own emotions. Life in this Moon will be sedate, or at least more so than usual. Lethargy is a common complaint, but is less common in this Moon than in a Taurus Moon.

Since you are so deeply emotional, and this is a safe Moon, take a hard and detailed look at yourself. Which direction do you want to take with your life? Why is it not headed that way? What are your long-term goals and what stops you from achieving them? What do you want to be when you grow up and why is it taking so long?

This Moon provides the perfect backdrop for detailed self-analysis and the close examination of your relationships. Your intuitive powers will assist you.

Bob, the husband of a close friend, often talks about his desire to strike out on his own in a completely different field of work. This Moon helps Bob to plan for his transition and make "real" choices about timing and the future.

This is a hard-working Moon and to feel comfortable in it you will have to work. Your intuition is available to help with the internal processes.

Scorpio Moon Personality in the Libra Moon

The airy Libra Moon will influence you to be a little scatter-brained, but that is the extent of its negative energy. This Moon is very loving and caring, and promotes sensitivity to other people's feelings.

In your dealings with others you might find yourself excessively concerned for their feelings. Your intuition will sort through these concerns and determine the difference between your fears of hurting their feelings and the reality of doing so. Take a look at the fears that come up because they may be a manifestation of your own security issues.

This Moon will act on you gently, as if to influence you with a caressing touch. This is a weak Moon that is unable to combat your inner strength and willpower. The only exception is its ability to scatter your focus. The Libra Moon is well versed in making a person unsure about their emotional state.

Scorpio Moon Personality in the Scorpio Moon

A Scorpio Moon personality in a Scorpio Moon transit can be compared to taking off your sunglasses to look directly at the Sun. This Moon will add intensity to your already intense emotional self.

You will require much from other people and expect them to stand clear. If you are in an adoring primary relationship, then your sensuality will come into play. Let this be the catalyst for a romantic evening with your favorite person. (Two of my friends, who are a couple, become lustfully passionate in this Moon.) If you are insecure with your mate, your jealousy and possessiveness could flare at any minute. Before you cut loose with a barrage, listen to and trust your intuition. You are probably just feeling the negative effects of this Moon. In reality you probably are adored, but possibly not in the manner that you would prefer.

Use the intensity of this Moon to make improvements. Try to rein in your negative feelings until life returns to some form of normalcy.

Scorpio Moon Personality in the Sagittarius Moon

You have an innate need for freedom from emotional ties in your life. Relationships are very important to your peace of mind, but you also need to feel independent, and to be free from clinging emotional relationships. The Sagittarius Moon is a freedom-loving Moon that looks at life as a carefree day on the beach.

This should be a good blend of energies for you. The Fire energy of this Moon will keep you on the move. The emotional freedom fostered by both Moons will give you permission to enjoy yourself. A couple of days in the sunshine will do you good.

I recommend downtime for people with Scorpio Moons in the Fire Moons. I have seen that my Scorpio Moon friends require regular recharging. The intensity that their Moon brings to their lives can quickly become overpowering.

The danger in this Moon is the total abandonment of responsibilities and commitments. You are far too sensitive to abandon another person but be aware that others could feel that they are being abandoned under certain circumstances. You don't have to physically run away because mental and emotional freedom are what you really desire.

Scorpio Moon Personality in the Capricorn Moon

This Earth Moon is practical. When influenced by this Moon you will be courageous, strong, willful, and driven to achieve. The Capricorn Moon is driven to succeed, but only when there is a personal stake in the outcome. This is not a Moon to try to accomplish something for someone else. You must be personally invested in the results.

This Moon will have a calming effect on your usual intensity. The grounding nature of this Moon will drain some of that passion, and help you to assert yourself without becoming upset. This is a Moon to work on your emotional ties with earthly ideals and items.

The abundance of self-storage businesses these days speaks to the growing number of pack rats that our society is breeding. This is a great time to cut the ties that bind you to unused "stuff." In the course of one Capricorn Moon transit, I visited three garage sales, each at the house of a Scorpio Moon friend.

Scorpio Moon Personality in the Aquarius Moon

The Aquarius Moon can bring a host of unfamiliar circumstances. It is a Moon that can lead you to believe that you have no emotions and that you don't need them. This Air Moon can be unpredictable and inconsistent. If you pretend that you have no emotions, those emotions will remain hidden, and there's no telling where or when they will erupt.

You may be prone to depression or withdrawal during this Moon. The depth at which you feel your emotions is only matched by the depth at which the Aquarius Moon persona tries to hide them. In order to sort out his feelings, Bob would go to the woods by himself for several days every few months. His wife and I looked at the dates he chose and found they almost always coincided with the Aquarius Moon.

This Moon will improve communication skills but care must be taken not to give the impression of insensitivity. This is unlikely, but at times you can be very matter-of-fact, and when mixed with the anesthetized feelings of the Aquarius Moon, insensitivity could result. If you are flexible in your approach to others, you will get along just fine.

Scorpio Moon Personality in the Pisces Moon

The Pisces Moon is a Moon of idealism when it come to emotions and relationships. In this Water Moon, your emotions will be the focus, but in the realm of the perfect relationship, the perfect romantic encounter, or the perfect lover.

You will feel better about your primary relationship (and about yourself), unless your primary relationship is not headed in the right direction. If that is the case, there will be some emotions to work through regarding your level of commitment.

This is a wonderful Moon if you are in the right place with the right person. Life will be sweet, and you may find yourself planning to build the cottage with the white picket fence. Improve your relationship with your partner. The romanticism of this Moon will help to soften both sides.

This Moon can also be used to improve your relationship with yourself. Reward yourself for efforts to overcome recent difficulties. Make some plans for your future. Create in your mind the vision of the perfect relationship, the perfect house, or the perfect life. Use affirmations to help bring these idealistic creations to fruition. This will be especially effective on a new Moon.

Sagittarius Moon

Your Lunar Profile

Sagittarius is the ninth sign of the Zodiac. Its planetary ruler is Jupiter, the heavenly father of the Roman civilization. In astrology, the planet Jupiter is associated with the material world and luck. It is Masculine and has the attributes of Fire.

You are an inspirational leader. You empower others by teaching them with encouragement. The pursuit of knowledge is a major life role for you, and this quest will often take you into the philosophical and religious realms. Your confidence in the cycle of life and the way it flows instills confidence in others.

You are idealistic, especially where your emotions are concerned. The utopian view of the world seen through your emotional filters can cause difficulties due to your expectations of others. Discretion can be a challenge, especially when another person does not meet your demands. It's hard for you to keep your feelings to yourself. You can unintentionally be very blunt and hurtful in your statements.

The Sagittarius Moon inspires you to be free of constraints. You strive to be independent and cannot stand to feel trapped or smothered. You are also very optimistic. Care should be taken to not let your optimism evolve into excessive idealism. If things don't work out the way you hope, you may begin to feel the walls of commitment closing in. Once you feel trapped, you start to make travel plans.

You have a good sense of humor and the ability to overlook your own failures. Laughing at yourself is a skill that you have mastered. Optimism and enthusiasm allow you to overcome failure. It's unlike you to question why you failed. You simply start over again and have faith that whatever you are trying to do will work out. You have a vision of what you want and where you want to go, and want to have fun while achieving your goals. Enthusiasm and the love of adventure keep you coming back for more.

Influences on the Sagittarius Moon Personality

Sagittarius Moon Personality in the Aries Moon

This Fire Moon will add anxiety and exhilaration to your carefree and romantic feelings. This is a time for action. It doesn't matter where you are going, only that you are going fast. You will want to be first in line, first at the traffic light, and will race to answer the phone.

You may become irritated with others who don't share your point of view. In this Moon, irritation can quickly turn to anger. Your emotions will be hotter than usual, especially those centered around confrontational issues.

My old friend, Nancy, and I have argued more times during an Aries Moon than in all other Moons combined. In fact, we rarely argue at any other time but during an Aries Moon. I remember an occasion when I called her and we had a disagreement before the first sentence was out of my mouth.

This could also be a very productive Moon. Use this motivational energy to get some things done. You would be best served to work on solo projects. Your impatience with others will only get in your way right now. They may not work efficiently enough or in a way you prefer.

The Aries Moon is a good time to start one of those projects that you've been putting off for some time. There is a high level of energy available for innovative approaches and new outlooks. You are creative in an adventurous way, so the things that you have previously considered risky are now exciting and fun.

Sagittarius Moon Personality in the Taurus Moon

In this Moon you will either feel quite persevering or lethargic. This is a good Moon to work on projects that have already been started. This is a firmly grounded Moon in which you will be better able to deal with earthly matters. Your energy level could be dramatically reduced, especially when starting something new. Stick to tasks already in progress.

Your home will be important during this Moon. This is your sanctuary—your place of warmth and safety from the outside world. Security will be a major focus. If emotional security is lacking, a sudden need for security at home or in a relationship could be the outer manifestation of a fear of recognition, loneliness, or acceptance.

Nancy feels drained of energy in this Moon and prefers to spend some quiet time in the confines of her house. It is difficult to coax her out during the Taurus Moon. She prefers to stay at home and play cards or board games.

Sagittarius Moon Personality in the Gemini Moon

Fickle, fun-loving, frolicsome, and flighty best describe the influences of the Gemini Moon. The Twins will sway you toward a multifaceted image. You will keep your inner-self somewhat hidden while delving into souls of others. Under this Air Moon you may find others describing you as "lacking focus" or "being scattered."

The Gemini Moon is an intellectual Moon, while the Sagittarius Moon is a romantic one. You will be bored unless an activity arouses your intellectual and sensual faculties. This is a time to move in social circles. You will be hardpressed to focus long enough to begin or complete any project which requires a concentrated effort.

Have some fun in this Moon—flirt and play. Try not to take this Moon too seriously. Allow yourself the freedom to be scattered. If you concentrate on your emotions, you will find it easier to connect with others.

Sagittarius Moon Personality in the Cancer Moon

The Cancer Moon will turn your focus inward. This Water Moon is very hard to ignore. This is a time of honesty with the self. The Cancer Moon will give you clear insight that allows you to see exactly what's occurring in your inner-world. If your emotional affairs are in order and you've been honestly dealing with them, then this Moon can be a happy one in which you will be able to work towards making your house a real home.

Clear insight comes from the Cancer Moon's ability to strip away all the ego-based rationales that you use to hide from the truth. The naked truth is all that remains and, if you have been dishonest with yourself, the naked truth can be harsh. You cannot avert your eyes from the inner-self during this transit.

The watery nature of this Moon will bring out your true feelings and fears, while its Fire augments their intensity and adds to the mix. It's not uncommon to feel trapped in this Moon—that there is no way out of your emotional prison. Although this isn't true, it is a real fear. My friend Nancy told me that she wanted to run to a retreat or the beach for a week whenever the tears of the Cancer Moon began to flow.

The secret is to not let your fears hold you back. You can see clearly now, so act to eliminate your fears without hesitation. Action towards resolution of your negative feelings is the best cure for the Cancer Moon.

Sagittarius Moon Personality in the Leo Moon

This Fire Moon can certainly make you feel good. The warmth of the Leo Moon is comfortable and promises a good time. You will be very sociable and outgoing, though you may become more interested in yourself than in the feelings of others.

The Lion is the King of the Jungle. You will want to be in charge, too. This fiery energy can make you pushy. Don't be surprised if you catch yourself issuing orders more frequently than is normal for you. Pride is another quality of this Moon that you will display in everything you do.

A sense of adventure may push you to try something new. Fear will not limit you in this Moon, so give it a whirl. You might have a good time, especially if you can share it with someone close to you.

The domestic scene will be comfortable as long as you remain in control, but don't be too domineering. There is a lot of energy in this Moon for family fun. Remember that others have emotional needs, too. Your support of their feelings will draw their emotional support to you.

Sagittarius Moon Personality in the Virgo Moon

The Virgo Moon is a critical Moon. It may inspire you to dissect the work, the personality, and the motivation of others. You will look into their very souls and dissect them to discover who they are and why they do what they do. While conducting this exploratory surgery, you won't only examine your findings but are likely to critique what you see. In your belief that your judgments are correct, you will form opinions about their performance, looks, or thoughts based on your perceptions.

It is safe to say that most people will not appreciate your analysis, criticism, or innate ability to present your opinions in a point-blank manner. Be aware of your opinions and your approach to others. You understand your friends' needs and how harsh or soft you must be with them. Respect these boundaries. One friend who helped to edit this book became quite exacting in the Virgo Moon. I expect my friends to tell me what they think, and to lay it on the line. The critique was straightforward, at times harsh, and completely appreciated.

This Moon can be very productive if you apply your critical abilities to yourself. Look into your inner-self and question what you claim to be. You may find that you are opinionated in an attempt to hide from yourself those traits that you feel are negative and unacceptable. By becoming less judgmental of yourself, you will be less judging of others.

Sagittarius Moon Personality in the Libra Moon

Your social skills improve in this Moon. Discussions with your inner-self will also be on a higher plane. The Libra Moon is a lovely Moon for your personality.

This Air Moon will decrease your decisiveness and reduce your willingness to begin new things or be impulsive. You will be well received by others and can win them over with your charm. You will be unwilling to let disharmony upset this tranquil existence, and you will put little energy into conflict. Your level of energy won't be affected but you won't need to be so outgoing or fiery. A warm calmness will better suit you in this Moon. Avoid your affinity for hot excitement.

A romantic interlude sounds promising in the Libra Moon. Your passionate nature will mix well with this Moon's romanticism. This is certainly a good time to improve your relationship with yourself. You will be very self-aware in this Moon and willing to honestly assess what you see.

Sagittarius Moon Personality in the Scorpio Moon

The Scorpio Moon will bring intensity to your personality. All the natal traits surrounding emotional involvement with others will be magnified.

Romance will be on your mind, but only if you can have it your way. You will want others to be flexible, loving, and supportive of your desires. You may expect your mate to toe the line—you have absolutely no tolerance for even the appearance of interest in others. If your significant other's focus should shift from you to another for even a short time, your jealousy will flare and strike like a lightning bolt.

I was stuck by this lightning a couple of times while dating a Sagittarius Moon girlfriend. Like lightning, her reaction came quickly, without warning, and vanished with only a rumbling in the distance.

You will use your charm and charisma to get what you want. If that doesn't work you may be very hard on yourself. On the other hand, if their response is better then predicted, sexual adventures could result. In any event, try to be a bit more mellow, which will greatly enhance your joy.

Sagittarius Moon Personality in the Sagittarius Moon

A nice warm home is always a comfortable place to be. You will be most like your natal self when the Moon is in Sagittarius. Others appreciate your good sense of humor and your genuine interest keeps them coming back. Your social skills are at their peak. Take advantage of them and enjoy your friendships.

Your adventurous side will show itself, especially if the adventure involves uncharted waters. Your thirst for new experiences and knowledge always pushes you to your limits.

Freedom, romance, and laughter will be yours. Don't be careless or insensitive, and all will be well. Be your happy self and enjoy life.

Sagittarius Moon Personality in the Capricorn Moon

This is the most secure Moon in the Zodiac. Capricorn is a well-grounded Earth sign and the Moon's influence in this sign will be toward finding security in your material and financial worlds. Emotional security, or the lack thereof, will be a byproduct of your relationship with the material world. If you are happy and content with your current financial status, you will probably feel more emotionally secure in this Moon. On the other hand, if you are not feeling good about your financial world, you could very likely feel insecure about your emotional world. This Moon translates earthy awareness into emotional contentment.

This is a good Moon in which to concentrate on things in which you are invested. Your focus on the betterment of your material world will keep you going. It won't satisfy you to work for the avarice of others or at your own expense.

Sagittarius Moon Personality in the Aquarius Moon

Emotional disappointment could cause you to question your comfort with a carefree lifestyle. Your natal ability to be carefree and easygoing is based on the assumption that life follows its regular course without intervention. In the Aquarius Moon, your emotions will be hidden deep inside. Life without emotions is idealistic and idealism is often slammed by reality. A complete commitment to all you do will subvert disillusion. Complete involvement draws out emotions and puts them to work. If you make a commitment to enjoy life, it will enhance your lifestyle and create the freedom to be carefree and easygoing.

You undermine your ability to be open with others if you suppress your emotions. Emotional accessibility allows you to connect with other people. Others will back away if you allow this Air Moon to hide your emotions behind meaningless chatter. Make the effort to stay emotionally involved.

Intellectually, you are well placed in this Moon. Your wits will be a match for any challenge. The secret is to allow others to mentally stimulate you by listening very closely. This could also be a challenge for you because the Air in this Moon may inspire you to chit-chat rather than converse.

Sagittarius Moon Personality in the Pisces Moon

The romance of the Pisces Moon coupled with the passionate heat of your Sagittarius Moon will be a very compatible, alluring, and possibly dangerous combination. You may find yourself planning a romantic weekend at some out-of-the-way spot for you and your sweetheart, such as an intriguing adventure to an undiscovered beach or a romantic country chalet. This is a time to make unforgettable memories. I've shared some very romantic moments under the Pisces Moon.

Traveling by yourself or even watching the sunset from your favorite restaurant's deck can bring extraordinary changes in your life. Under the spell of this very romantic Moon, you could become quickly and blindly involved in a heated romance that lasts a few days or much longer. Once the heat of the moment wears off, you will be able to judge your compatibility. Regardless, you will have memories of a wonderful romantic interlude.

Capricorn Moon

Your Lunar Profile

The sign of Capricorn is the tenth sign of the Zodiac. It is a Feminine, Earth sign, ruled by Saturn. "Practicality" is the key word for this Moon and applies to the emotional world as well as the physical world. You are most comfortable when life is structured and work best with guidelines and preset goals. You can organize any activity into a simple step-by-step process which virtually guarantees success.

A sense of order in your life is a prerequisite for self-confidence and security. When you have things well organized you can accomplish almost anything. Your emotions, however, will not submit to such extreme organization. In fact, the only way to keep your emotions in order is to hide your inner-self from everyone, including yourself. Unfortunately, insecurity is often the result.

One of the reasons why your practical nature operates in opposition to your emotions is your natal sign. The sign of Capricorn is opposite from Cancer in the Zodiac. Since the Moon is associated with Cancer and rules your emotional inner-self, your Capricorn Moon may influence you to repress your emotions rather than to show the world your true self.

If you keep your emotions under tight reins in order to feel safe, others will perceive you to be cold and insensitive. It will be difficult for you to connect with other people, because a true connection to others requires intimacy, which is gained through sharing emotions. Not only will you find it hard to display your emotions and share your feelings, but you will be critical of others who do. Criticism leads to judgement, and judgement is often a strategy for not facing our fears.

The best remedy for emotional insecurity is to learn to deal with your own emotional and spiritual needs. Bring your emotions out into the open and examine them. Learn to admit to yourself how you really feel about things. You are a sensitive person and your feelings can be hurt easily. You are more vulnerable if you hide your feelings. Allow yourself to share your hurts and your joys with others and you will find them less painful and your friends more supportive.

Your intuition can boost your emotional security. You are very likely to ignore your inner feelings and warnings as impractical fears rather than insightful, instinctual information. Deep down, you know that you are a good, trustworthy person. You also know when you are in a dangerous or life-threatening situation.

Those jealous of your success will describe you as materialistic. Actually, you are discriminating in your tastes. Your possessions show a certain style and "class." Patience is one of your many virtues. It is your resolute patience that allows you to delay a purchase until it's for sale at the price you want to pay. If you cannot find what you want or cannot find it at the right price, you won't buy it.

You are sensible in your approach to life. Others will look to you for structure, advice, and help. When others cannot get the job done, you can show them the path and even lead the way. Ambition is one of your motivating factors. You work tirelessly to achieve any goal in which you have a personal stake.

Influences on the Capricorn Moon Personality

Capricorn Moon Personality in the Aries Moon

The Fire of this Moon will release your inhibitions. Although you are usually reserved and control your emotions, this Moon may find a crack in your armor and release those desires that you have been holding back for so long. Emotional spontaneity might be what's needed to fulfill some of those romantic fantasies. Once this Moon gets your motor running, let yourself go and experience life in the fast lane.

The first time Jim walked on fire with me was under the Aries Moon. I had offered him every opportunity to attend my firewalks, but he always declined. Not so mysteriously, the energy of the Aries Moon helped him to change his mind. He arrived at the firewalk with a glow in his eyes, ready to fully participate.

The heat of this Moon will be widespread. You are already hard-working and very practical, and this will be a particularly productive time. Under the fiery influence of the Aries Moon you may be inclined to start new projects, to take risks, and to break the bonds of financial and emotional security.

Your temper could be hot, or at least shorter than usual. The cool-headed Capricorn Moon does not lose its temper easily. The Fire in this Moon will weaken those restraints and increase your emotional volatility.

Capricorn Moon Personality in the Taurus Moon

The Taurus Moon complements your earthy qualities. This Moon will bring feelings of security and stability to your life. Materialism is more predominant in this Moon. Your drive to accomplish things will be enhanced, but your speed out of the starting blocks will be reduced.

The Taurus Moon can certainly influence you to be a workhorse, and you will be most productive when completing projects. You will most likely resemble "a bull in a china shop" if you try to start a new project because you can easily become frustrated with details and people. The stubbornness of the Bull will cause tempers to flare.

This is a great opportunity to kick back and relax, and to surround yourself with beauty. A gorgeous place in nature is your best bet. A dreary hotel room or dingy apartment would be a difficult locale for relaxation, at best.

Don't be surprised if you feel sexy right now. Open up to your erotic side and have some fun. You are more forward than usual and more willing to say what's on your mind. Be direct when approaching others and don't be afraid of embarrassment.

Capricorn Moon Personality in the Gemini Moon

You may be feeling as though your personality has been split. Your basic personality is one of consistency and stability, but in this Moon you will be easily persuaded to change your plans. You are not comfortable with fickle behavior, which will lead you to question yourself and your motives.

Your creative abilities will peak in the Gemini Moon. The constraints of your focused intellect are removed by this Moon. Your structured approach to reasoning is transformed and expanded—you may look at many options, including those which seem illogical and nonsensical. Your imagination will be bolstered by the strange energies of this Moon.

Take this opportunity to look at troubling situations in your life. This Gemini Moon will help you to see things from a totally different point of view. Stay open to the perspectives offered for your review. You will find that there are other ways to approach life than through rigid, logical reasoning.

Capricorn Moon Personality in the Cancer Moon

This Water Moon will prompt you to look at your inner-self. You will recognize your emotional needs and pinpoint the relationships which are working and the ones which are struggling. Although this sounds simple, you seldom are conscious of the blinders you wear. The Cancer Moon allows you to see the difficulties you bring to relationships by removing the blinders,.

Jim describes himself as "very sensitive." I find this to be especially true in the Cancer Moon. It didn't take me long to figure out that teasing Jim in a Cancer Moon was a bad idea.

The Cancer Moon will help you to strip away the composed facade which you so proudly display in favor of an uncensored look at the true you. This can be a very scary process, but it's also an enlightening and gratifying one. Take this opportunity to push your boundaries. Let others, especially those with whom you are close, see a part of you that has been deeply hidden. If you share your innermost thoughts and feelings with your closest companion, it will bring a greater level of intimacy than ever before.

Your challenge is to allow yourself to experience intimacy through confiding in others. This won't happen if others have to drag it out of you. This Moon will give you a start. Use it to discover the wonderfully passionate person hiding behind all that logic.

Capricorn Moon Personality in the Leo Moon

The heat of this Fire Moon will bring your thoughts back to yourself and how you believe that others perceive you. You will want to open up to others due to your desire to be seen as a caring, nurturing, and loving soul. Fears of being judged negatively will hold you back. These fears could also make you more short-tempered than would otherwise be true.

You seek recognition rather than intimacy in this Moon. The Leo Moon likes to be noticed—positive recognition is best but any recognition will do. When you choose to withdraw rather than express your feelings, recognition from others or standing in the spotlight may make you feel uneasy. The Leo Moon will ask you to showcase your emotions.

After talking with me about the influence of the Moon on his basic personality, Jim decided to throw a party one Leo Moon evening. Many friends and acquaintances came. Jim was suddenly the center of attention—telling jokes, laughing, and confessing many things he's done that he considers to be foolish or stupid. With every story, the party's energy level rose. The Moon's influence helped Jim to connect with his own emotional wellspring.

The turmoil that you feel about exposing your emotions may be expressed as anger. Your Capricorn lunar influences are very strong—you know exactly where the boundaries of your comfort zone lie. The Leo Moon's intense energy will push you to the edge and urge you to jump.

Capricorn Moon Personality in the Virgo Moon

This Moon is back in your comfort zone, and may feel like returning home after a long vacation. The Virgo Moon is an Earth Moon that complements your Moon and will influence you to bury your emotions.

Life's details will call to you. Handle the particulars that impede your progress, especially in activities that hold a special interest for you.

Martyrdom may be a hidden motivation for dealing with onerous details. It's difficult to express how you feel when others don't do their fair share or are unwilling to deal with minutia. You may slip into a cycle of passive revenge. It is undeniably convenient to imagine that by doing the work yourself others will feel bad. If you express your feelings more readily, you will easily avoid this cycle of resentment and revenge.

Capricorn Moon Personality in the Libra Moon

Your emotions are not an open book, but examination of the inner-self is a real possibility. Lunar Libran energies help you be less reticent. Self-assessments will be less harsh in this Moon.

You will be more personable. You are more likely to connect with others because you will be more compassionate. Your charitable analysis of others will hook them and your charm will reel them in.

Your romantic side may sneak out. The Libra Moon could be a great time to work on your relationships, especially relationships of the heart. You will not find another Moon so approachable and so generous with charm. Let your true self shine and the those around you will smile. It's hard to say "no" to my friend Jim when his charm is working for him. He just has a way of getting others to agree with him.

Capricorn Moon Personality in the Scorpio Moon

Your intuitive abilities and psychic powers will be more intense. You would be well advised to use these powers to your best advantage. This requires opening yourself to your feelings and instincts. You are a "real world" person, and this strange attraction to your psychic nature makes you uncomfortable. By allowing yourself to tune into another "world" your understanding of the hidden aspects of any situation will become extremely accurate and complete. This comprehensive and unerring ability to see what's hidden will also work to see your inner-self. The real test is trusting your "feelings."

The Scorpio Moon is a passionate Water Moon. Your reactions to it will probably be intense. Passion is pervasive and addictive—it affects all aspects of your life. You will find yourself drawn to the passion of this Moon, especially if you are involved in a romantic relationship.

Capricorn Moon Personality in the Sagittarius Moon

The Sagittarius Moon is a Fire Moon with quite a playful streak. Take a couple of days off and enjoy. Fun and frolic are its two primary directives. If it's not easy or exciting it's not worth doing. Let go of earthly bonds. You might get used to the freedom of an easygoing lifestyle. I once attended another instructor's firewalk under a Sagittarius Moon. I spotted a car in the parking lot, owned by a Capricorn Moon person, that had an appropriate bumper sticker, "If it's not fun, don't do it."

One way to spoil this fun is to focus on your finances. It is easy to deny yourself pleasure if you are concerned about money or work. Stay out of the patterns that keep you in your comfort zone and deny you the pleasures that life has to offer.

The unrestrained energies of this Moon may make you feel uneasy as you open up to them. This will pass with time. Just enjoy the freedom of being the person you want to be instead of the person you show everyone else.

Capricorn Moon Personality in the Capricorn Moon

This is an excellent opportunity to complete important projects. The influence of this Moon will simply be to enhance your basic emotional traits and characteristics. You will probably feel well and be in a good mood. You will also be extremely productive. Pursue those lifelong goals and ambitions.

This is the lunar energy of a workaholic. Avoid completely withdrawing into work. Playtime is important to even the most intelligent and motivated people. If you allow yourself to withdraw into your work, it will affect the other people in your life. They want to share in the things you do—in your joys and sorrows. It is important in this Moon to involve others in your life. You will benefit from the resulting intimacy.

Capricorn Moon Personality in the Aquarius Moon

This Moon's effect on your emotional responses will be unpredictable. There will be moments when everything seems fine, but at times you will be disappointed by unrealistic expectations. As with the other Air Moons, you will be more flighty and less focused than usual. Life will not follow its normal path. There will be many distractions along the way that make it difficult to be centered and to maintain your balance. The Aquarius Moon will bring out your idealistic tendencies, while appealing to your earthy nature. Emotional investiture in these ideals will throw you off balance if they fail to materialize.

Lessen your load, continue life with less self-importance. Don't get too serious. You are basing your performance on goals which cannot be attained. Pursue quick and easy goals for now and have some fun.

Capricorn Moon Personality in the Pisces Moon

The astrological cycle ends with this Moon and begins with the next—symbolizing death and rebirth. It is time to rethink, replan, and reorganize. Develop new structures and strategies after careful consideration of your past performance. You may find yourself withdrawing from the front lines for a short time while you realign your efforts to match with your new goals.

This is also a good time for introspection. Don't underestimate the power of this Water Moon. It can take what you see as practical and turn it on you if you are not emotionally secure. Look deep inside and use this Moon to evaluate your emotional performance while you critique your professional performance. This Moon will promote self-acceptance and self-love. All you need is honesty.

Jim makes a list of things he wants to accomplish each month during the Pisces Moon. He feels he doesn't get anything done without a list. Every month he updates his list, re-evaluates the items left undone, and prioritizes life's new challenges.

Another quality of this Water Moon is romance. This is the premier romantic Moon. An outpouring of emotion is a possibility even for the well-grounded Capricorn. Don't hold back.

Aquarius Moon

Your Lunar Profile

Aquarius is the eleventh sign in the Zodiac. It is a Masculine, Air sign ruled by the planet Uranus, which is the planet of inspiration and creativity. You are a friendly person, though you find it difficult to be intimate save with a select few. You tend to be idealistic and are involved in humanitarian activities. Freedom is important. You are thoughtful and protective of others' freedom as well. You are imaginative, inventive, and even inspired at times.

Your innate friendliness is one of your most endearing characteristics. People respond well to your unusual ability to connect with others and draw them out. Conventionality is not one of your strong points. Your relationships will be a little different or out of the ordinary. You are a great friend.

Idealism pervades all areas of your life. In love relationships you desire the fairy-tale romance. Unfortunately, the world we live in can be cynical, making the "perfect romance" almost unattainable. When a relationship doesn't meet your idealistic goals, you may begin to shift from romance to friendship. Although you are interested in romantic relationships, you feel that it's easier to deal with friends than lovers because a lower level of emotional commitment is required. You hold your emotions deep within and are reluctant to expose yourself to anything less than the fairy-tale romance.

Passion is an absolute necessity. Some astrologers have said that Aquarius Moon personalities tend to be less passionate in their relationships. This is not true. Friendship is a very important part of a love relationship and this is where you concentrate your attention. Once you consider the friendship a success and feel safe to express your emotions, you allow yourself to show intense passion.

Humanitarianism is an idealistic approach to life and you become firmly entrenched in it. Setting high, hard-to-reach goals is wonderfully productive. You have a way of enlisting individual support and networking with the business community. These qualities create success: you achieve your goals, give individuals and businesses a sense of community, and work for the greater good.

Freedom is of great importance to you. The ability to able to do what you want with whomever you want is a freedom that you require in any love relationship. This can make for some rather unconventional relationships. You are also a great protector of other people's freedom and demonstrate this in your relationships. Many people talk about having an open, honest, and free relationship but few can achieve it. You not only achieve it but consider it important to a relationship's success.

This Air Moon makes you less focused than other Moons. The advantages include a less rigid and more flexible nature that fuels creativity and imagination. You don't let conventions control your thoughts. Your independence makes you somewhat of a mystery to others, yet these qualities draw them to you. They are attracted by your friendly nature, charisma, and exhilaration with life.

You are a friendly person but don't let others see the real you. They will like what they see. Let yourself open up to others.

Influences on the Aquarius Moon Personality

Aquarius Moon Personality in the Aries Moon

This Fire sign is the first sign in the Zodiac. It has the power to help you to initiate activities. You will feel good about starting a new project and will commit the emotional energy necessary.

You may find yourself on edge. This fiery Moon will heat up your feelings. You will be less apathetic and more adversarial. Controversy will occur more frequently if your emotions are bottled up inside. Whatever upsets or irritates you will be brought to the surface by this Moon. If you are hiding from your emotions, be careful in this Moon.

Restrictions on your freedom will be a hot topic. Nothing will set you off like someone trying to restrict your options or dictate your actions. Should you find yourself faced with a loss of freedom, remember that you always have the right to choose.

Aquarius Moon Personality in the Taurus Moon

A strong Earth Moon can have a profound influence on your emotions. You may feel more secure, which will make it easier for you to be affectionate. The Taurus Moon will have such an influence on you because it fosters feelings of security.

You will easily hold others at bay. The Taurus Moon provides an unyielding influence. You will not be easily swayed to change your mind. You will be successful at helping others to see your point.

Mike is a general foreman in construction. I had an opportunity to spend a day with him and was amazed at the apparent complete shift in his personality from work to home. In the Taurus Moon he was unyielding and powerful on the job, and he persuaded others to adopt his point of view. When we arrived at home, he became so tender and affectionate with his family that I barely recognized him.

This is a good time to work on things already started. An endeavor that you may have started with the energy of the Aries Moon is a good target for the stubbornness and dedication of the Taurus Moon.

Aquarius Moon Personality in the Gemini Moon

Gemini is an Air Moon. In this mutable Moon you will rediscover the gift of gab. The airy energies of this Moon will draw out your talkative and friendly personality. The duality of this sign is reflected in your emotions. You are likely to show the world a self-assured persona, while holding back that with which you are least secure.

This is a good time to get out and talk to people. Any format for personal interaction is appropriate. Enjoy your friends, throw a party, or attend one. Mike, who has an Aquarius Moon, came to a party at my house during a Gemini Moon transit. He immediately became the center of attention. His innate charm and talkative personality often make Mike the life of the party.

This is not a time to make emotional commitments or, for that matter, commitments of any kind. You will be better served to leave heavy, intense relationships off your list of things to do. This is not the Moon to enter into a physical relationship with anyone. Any emotional commitment made at this time may feel like a loss of freedom.

Things begun in this Moon will typically not last. The staying power of the Gemini Moon is almost nonexistent. Despite the best of intentions, emotional or earthly matters initiated in this Moon are destined to fail.

Try to take things less seriously. Your communication skills are supercharged right now, so take advantage of them. Make your friends and family a priority.

Aquarius Moon Personality in the Cancer Moon

The Cancer Moon is a Water Moon, which will help you look at your emotional strengths and weaknesses. This could be a fairly comfortable Moon if you are willing to be honest about your feelings. If you are lying to yourself, this Moon will remind you that all is not forgotten.

This Moon has been traditionally known as the Moon of ever-changing moods. In some ways your airy nature increases the effects of this Moon because you don't focus long on a single effort. Your mood will change as your focus changes and your emotions respond to the new circumstances. This can be an asset because shifting emotional gears keeps you from being overwhelmed.

There will be times when you will be totally carefree and times when you totally lose control of your emotions. It all depends on your level of self-knowledge, as well as the intensity of any repressed emotions. The Cancer Moon can be very comfortable. All you need is a willingness to express your feelings. As you are increasingly able to handle your emotions, the influence of the Cancer Moon decreases.

Aquarius Moon Personality in the Leo Moon

This Fire sign will focus your attention on yourself and the image you hold out to others. You will want your deeds to be noticed and will become more outgoing to accomplish that goal. Your emotional needs will not be a priority in this Moon; however, if your need for recognition is not being met, you will quickly become emotional. You may use those emotions to persuade others to recognize your accomplishments.

As a general foreman for a construction company, part of Mike's job is to wheel and deal with the other contractors to create opportunities for his crew. He is very good at his job. In a Leo

Moon, Mike is unsurpassed in displaying just the right balance of personable influence and assertiveness.

Your personality will be bolstered by the heat of this Moon. Although you are very personable and eloquent during this Moon, your personality will shine even brighter. You will benefit if you use these qualities to pursue firmly established goals.

The Leo Moon is your opposite in the Zodiac and will have a tendency to challenge you. At times it will be difficult to keep this Moon from dragging you down. Its fiery influences should help combat these effects by adding energy. The negative side might be an increased capacity for anger. Be careful to be positive and to enjoy the Sun.

Aquarius Moon Personality in the Virgo Moon

This Moon will ask you to look at the details of life. This conflicts with your airy nature, which is not conducive to detailed work over long periods of time. In some respects, this Moon will help. The Virgo Moon will give you the emotional drive you need to tackle details; however, you may find this newfound desire to be short-lived. If you are forced to examine your every action or emotion, you may become frustrated. You may feel a loss in personal freedom if others examine, critique, or gossip about you.

Avoid forging new relationships. You will not easily accept scrutiny and may find it difficult to not criticize others. If you are in a situation that requires detailed analysis, you couldn't pick a better Moon for the task.

This Moon is best spent focusing on yourself. The analytical powers of the Virgo Moon will improve self-examination. Don't be too hard on yourself; remember the old adage about not seeing the forest for the trees.

Aquarius Moon Personality in the Libra Moon

In many ways this Air Moon will be very comfortable for you. It emphasizes communication and interaction with others, and in this you are well versed and very relaxed.

The emotional tranquility of this Moon is conducive to honest self-assessment, which increases your ability and willingness to display your true self to others. At first you may be uncomfortable, but you will have a sense of safety and security that allows you to the explore your inner world.

These favorable factors—peacefulness and emotional security—coupled with your communication skills, will add to the charm, sincerity, and romantic feeling of your relationships. If you permit others to see your true emotions, you will endear yourself to them. They will probably describe you as lovable, caring, and in touch with yourself.

Mike asked me to meet him for a beer one day after work. Halfway through our Hefeweizen, Mike thanked me for insisting that he would be best served if he was honest about his feelings with his wife, regardless of what he thought she might think. Mike said that communicating his feelings to his wife Karen brought them closer together.

You will not find a safer Moon to work on yourself or your primary relationships. Take this opportunity to explore and share your feelings. You will improve your relationship with yourself by improving the quality of your relationships.

Aquarius Moon Personality in the Scorpio Moon

The Scorpio Moon will bring passion to your life. It may increase your ability to trust in your psychic abilities. The Scorpio Moon will intensify any emotional issue.

This Moon has no regard for your ability to detach. It will force you to hear the call of the inner person. Any emotion that escapes from long-term bondage will greatly affect you. This release will ultimately be a step in a positive direction, but the immediate response to emotional freedom may feel negative. Since very few people hide joyful emotions, the emotions that are released are likely to be negative. Karen reported that since Mike has learned to open up to her, his emotional lows have become much less severe and less frequent.

The intensity of this Moon will affect your relationships. The Scorpio Moon's passionate energy pervasively affects all areas of your life. This Moon will enhance your feelings of love and adoration for your life partner as well as your physical desire.

Your ability to skillfully detach from your feelings will be no match for this Moon's straightforward, passionate influence. You will pine for what you previously craved and lust after what you previously desired. Every emotion will increase in magnitude.

Aquarius Moon Personality in the Sagittarius Moon

In this casual, warm Moon you will feel comfortable. Friendships flourish under the fiery Sagittarius Moon.

Your imagination will be enhanced. Your flights of fantasy will be fun for all concerned. The Sagittarius Moon is typically lighthearted. Make use of it to decompress from the day-to-day stresses.

Your need for independence will be as great as ever, but will seldom cause conflict. The Sagittarius Moon influences everyone to different degrees. Another positive aspect of this Moon is the faith you have in the process of life. If you feel that you are flowing in life's currents and know that all rivers ultimately flow to the ocean, rejoining the Great Mother, you can be secure in your independence and be confident in yourself. It feels good to let go and trust that you will arrive at your destination.

Romance is in the air. In the company of the right person, a romantic interlude is possible. You are usually not interested in a torrid affair. On the other hand, this warm, romantic Moon could provide the spark that transforms an initially casual attraction to a committed relationship. Show a little interest, and you will be pleasantly surprised at the other person's response.

Twice a month, Mike and Karen plan some time alone. They have wisely chosen the Sagittarius and Pisces Moons for their trysts. As a result of their intimate "retreats," they find that they will use any excuse to spend more time together. Once they went so far as to call in sick to work in order to visit a nearby spa, where they shared a sauna, a hot tub, and a massage.

Aquarius Moon Personality in the Capricorn Moon

The next few days could be a very solemn period for you. The emotional severity of your Moon will be amplified by the Capricorn Moon, but with a slightly different slant. You may find that the Capricorn Moon orients you toward the material world.

Almost everyone I know has taken to working on personal finance issues in this Moon. You will be attracted to structured activities. You will feel more disciplined. These traits are especially predominant when your goals are based in personal desire. This could be a very productive, unemotional Moon if you are personally invested in the fruits of your efforts.

This isn't a great time to work on relationships. The tendency to hide emotions is only enhanced by the Capricorn Moon. Security of all kinds, including emotional and financial security, will be a major focus. Emotional safety is instinctual.

Aquarius Moon Personality in the Aquarius Moon

This is your natal Moon sign. The unpredictability inherent in your Air sign will be magnified. Idealistic tendencies will surface in your decisions. You may set your heart on an outcome that is based on the mistaken perception that we live in a perfect world. This ever-changing world has its share of joyful surprises and shocking disappointments in store for you.

You are an independent thinker with a good imagination. These natal qualities are further enhanced by the Aquarius Moon. Your ability and willingness to listen to your instincts and intuition can bring much success. Your thoughts will be deemed unconventional by some because you use intuition to see the other side of a situation. The danger is in allowing idealism to slant the outcome. Be careful to temper your feelings with a realistic look at the circumstances.

Aquarius Moon Personality in the Pisces Moon

In the Pisces Moon you can recuperate and digest the month-long emotional journey that you have just completed. This Water Moon can be maudlin. You will look back at the good times that could have been, and those that were, and wish for more. All of this sentimentality is lessened by allowing yourself to experience emotions. Hiding emotion turns sentimentality to remorse.

The Pisces Moon is very romantic. Over the next few days you will have an opportunity to deeply connect with your life partner. Open up to your feelings and experience real joy. Don't expect the other person to just know what you are feeling. Tell them how you feel and enjoy the intimacy of honest emotional reflection.

This is a difficult time to hold a garage sale. It is almost impossible for me to give up my favorite things in this sentimental Moon.

Pisces Moon

Your Lunar Profile

Pisces is the last sign of the Zodiac. It is a Feminine, Water sign and is co-ruled by the planets Jupiter and Neptune. The Moon in Pisces gives you extremely strong intuitive abilities. You are also emotionally sensitive. Creativity and an artistic eye are of great benefit to you.

You are very intuitive and can be easily influenced by the emotional responses of others. Your empathy for the problems and difficulties of others can overload you. This ability can be a great strength when used wisely and under your control. If you overexpose yourself to negative emotions you may need to seek seclusion to protect yourself. You can be defenseless against an onslaught of psychological pressure from others. Always be aware of the degree to which you are open to the outside world.

By this time in life, you have probably learned to trust your instincts. Instinctual information is quite accurate if you are receptive to the truth. So many times, the information gleaned from intuitive sources is molded and shaped by desires.

You are extremely sensitive, and take others' opinions to heart. This makes you easily influenced and susceptible to the manipulation of others. You are the first to cry at movies, and disasters reported on the evening news can leave you distraught.

You are truly a hopeless romantic. Emotional sensitivity allows you to be more receptive to the words and deeds of others—you "feel" more deeply than the other Moon signs. This magnum level of sensory perception is confusing, especially in a romantic situation. It's very important to look at this person or prospective relationship with severe honesty. You can be idealistic, and if you live in this dream world for too long, you may delude yourself about the real world.

Take advantage of your intuitive abilities. Listen to your inner voice when first meeting someone. Your first impression will probably be accurate. In conversation, your inner voice speaks to you about that person's integrity.

Compassion is very strong in you. This is a wonderful quality but you must be careful not to let others take advantage of your compassionate nature. A heartfelt story might persuade you when logical means would not.

Spirituality is another of your admirable qualities. Emotional sensitivity easily connects you to your spirit. This connection is demonstrated through your intuition. Compassion plays a big part in your spirituality as well. All of these qualities are brought to fruition through your willingness to care about and help others. This is where your idealistic beliefs are of great benefit. If the world could be shaped in the perfect image of idealistic dreams, then you would be a true prophet.

Influences on the Pisces Moon Personality

Pisces Moon Personality in the Aries Moon

In this Fire Moon you will have more control over your emotions. The strong influences you receive from the Aries Moon engenders fierce independence. This, coupled with the feeling of independence you receive from your intuition, promotes a sense of freedom and self-reliance.

You may find yourself drawn to a challenge during this Moon, or may become bored with regimented activities. Start demanding and challenging projects that require a firm commitment. You are emotionally energized and better equipped to deal with emotional commitments and difficulties.

Your romantic energies are intensified. It's easier to relate to your partner, especially on the subject of amour. Those who attract you most in this Moon will probably be the most difficult to capture. Your mate could keep your undivided attention by pretending to be aloof and uninterested. Watch your needs closely and try not to get carried away with the pursuit of something or someone you only chase for the challenge.

Pisces Moon Personality in the Taurus Moon

The Taurus Moon is probably the most grounded Moon for the Pisces Moon personality. The Taurus Moon will add earthy stability to your emotions. You are apt to feel more secure in all aspects of your life, especially in your relationships. Emotional security spawns a safe opportunity to investigate and deal with otherwise emotionally charged issues. You are less likely to have your feelings hurt. Emotional work is easiest when the risk of injury is low.

Sabrina is an intuitive counselor and friend. Through an intuitive connection, enhanced by the Pisces Moon, her understanding of another person's feelings is clear and useful. In the Taurus Moon, Sabrina can handle anything I tell her. Much of her information comes from intuition—she "feels" what I feel. In other Moons, Sabrina is more likely to shed tears with me.

The Taurus Moon is not a time to start and finish anything that relies on a flash of intense energy. This Moon is slow and methodical. Things started now will be long-lasting and influential in your life. Use this to your advantage by putting desirable, new habits in place. Only begin what you want to become habitual.

This is a good time to commune with your life partner. You will desire closeness and affection. Take advantage of this chance for intimacy. A cozy evening in a quiet moonlit garden will do wonders for your love life.

Pisces Moon Personality in the Gemini Moon

The split personality of the Gemini Moon will cause you to experience a greater separation between your inner and outer-selves. In other words, you may want to conceal your emotions and to promote a certain ego-based image. This split in your personality could become very interesting. It will be a good opportunity to examine what you choose to hide from others. These are the things the ego tries to protect.

Communication will take on new importance. You may find yourself very interested in what others have to say. This feeling will be further amplified by your intuition, because you use it to judge a person's integrity.

One irritant of this Moon is the inability to stay focused on a given topic for an extended period of time. The airy influences of the Gemini Moon will cause you to be flighty in your thoughts and emotions. Don't be surprised if you contemplate a change in address or rearrange the furniture.

Pisces Moon Personality in the Cancer Moon

This Water Moon is comfortable for the Pisces Moon personality. The Cancer Moon will intensify your intuitive prowess.

You should feel strong emotionally. The domestic feeling of this Moon will add a sense of security and provide an opportunity to look inside and pinpoint emotional difficulties. Sensitive feelings indicate unresolved issues. Lower your defenses in order to examine the source of your insecurities.

Use your intuition in your dealings with others. This Moon will let you tune in to others at an unusually intense level. You will nurture the people closest to you. This will come from a deep, instinctual understanding of their emotional needs. These messages are always present, but you may not always be open to them. This Moon lowers the barriers, and allows you to make an intuitive connection.

Sabrina is very open during the Cancer Moon. She understands the story I relate even when I'm not very clear. In this Moon, she often becomes emotionally involved in my story. She empathically connects with me and "feels" what I am feeling.

Pisces Moon Personality in the Leo Moon

This Fire Moon will forge the strength of self-confidence. Your emotions will be held in check. You will be more confident and in control, due in part to your decreased dependence on others. Although connections with others are very important, you will focus on your own needs. Increased self-awareness, a feeling of security, and reduced emotional stresses breed self-confidence and control over your life.

You may want to brag about your accomplishments. This should not be too surprising because the Lion's energies will make you feel that you deserve to be at the center of attention. A friend of mine, Bill, has a Pisces Moon. He likes to beat his chest over his accomplishments, even the lucky ones, in the Leo Moon.

Do not run from love. This is a great Moon to rekindle the flames of romance in your relationship. Show your mate the fiery passion of Leo and you will be pleased with the results. The relationship will be fulfilling because your partner will reflect what is received from you. If you feel safe with your emotions, your partner will also feel safe. Your romantic feelings will impassion your mate and the love relationship you share. This is not a great time, however, to initiate a new romance in your life if you expect it to last. The Leo Moon's fiery energy makes lasting personal connections difficult.

Pisces Moon Personality in the Virgo Moon

This could be a trying Moon for you because Virgo is opposite your natal sign of Pisces. You may feel sluggish and depleted. The Virgo Moon is an Earth Moon which aids in the grounding of your energy reservoirs. With energy levels down, your emotions could take a beating. Be aware of your responses to outside stimuli. It's difficult to keep your shields up if you are feeling drained. ("Shields" refers to a process of surrounding yourself with white light as a block or shield against receiving incompatible or unacceptable energies from others.)

This Moon may influence you to be particular about almost everything, and may cause you to be detail-oriented. Your critical faculties may create difficult moments in relationships; however, self-analysis is easier to accomplish. You will not be as easily moved by the truth, be it good or bad. As a result, you can accept and understand reality.

If you have a detailed task to perform or need to be critical, this Moon will be a wonderful time to accomplish your goals. The "picky" nature of Virgo will support you and motivate you in these tasks.

Pisces Moon Personality in the Libra Moon

"Charm" and "personality" are the buzzwords for this Moon. Libra is an Air Moon and will have you talking with everybody. Your natural intuition will give you the insight to discern the true message of others while your charm and wit disarms them. This is a great Moon for furthering a relationship.

The Libra Moon is notorious for the inability to make decisions. For this reason, you may find spontaneity difficult. Once someone else has set the course, you will have no trouble following. A problem arises when Bill and I are together and neither of us can decide what to do or where to go. In a Libra Moon there are too many choices and too much time—we are useless.

The Libra Moon will have quite a romantic effect on you. You are a hopeless romantic anyway, and this Moon will emphasize this trait and throw in a good dose of charisma to really get things rolling. Take a weekend trip to a favorite romantic spot and work on your love relationship (but plan this vacation in the Taurus Moon).

You are extremely self-aware right now. Meditate on your inner strengths and weaknesses. Focusing on moments of emotional stress will pinpoint the real problem.

Pisces Moon Personality in the Scorpio Moon

The Scorpio Moon is an intense Water Moon, though you will feel almost as content as in your natal Moon. The difference will be passion. The Scorpio Moon will highlight that certain alluring magnetism which is sometimes hidden. You won't go unnoticed. You will have the complete attention of your mate.

Part of this attraction is caused by your heightened intuitive abilities. The ability to sense another's needs can be an attractive quality if used to your advantage. It's helpful to use your instinctual knowledge when extracting the real meaning from spoken words. Sometimes people have a hard time saying what they mean, or are too embarrassed to speak intimately.

Notice your strong reactions to emotional situations in the Scorpio Moon. Intensity is a Scorpio trademark. Emotions will be more pronounced than usual, which creates an opportunity to identify emotional difficulties. The increased magnitude will make it easier to distinguish subtle differences in your feelings and possibly relieve some confusion.

Pisces Moon Personality in the Sagittarius Moon

This is a congenial, upbeat Fire Moon. You won't experience a great deal of worry during this Moon. Instead, you have an opportunity to enjoy yourself. Kick back and relax, do what ever strikes your fancy. Throw a party or find one. Meet with friends and hang out.

A sense of connection with the general flow of things is important. You don't have the fortitude to buck the system during the Sagittarius Moon. It's best to follow the general direction in which life leads you. You always have options—right now it's just easiest to sit back and let life happen.

You may feel uncomfortable in lively group situations. Although this Moon will bring out the extrovert hidden deep within, you may be uncomfortable. You see yourself as an inwardly focused person. Try to let go. You will be the life of the party if you turn yourself loose.

Pisces Moon Personality in the Capricorn Moon

Material security, structure, and practical matters will concern you in this Moon. If you are already in a secure lifestyle, you will probably feel comfortable; if not, you may feel very ill at ease. Be active in pursuing your goals at home and with your personal finances.

This isn't the best time for a romantic interlude. You may feel too calculating for spontaneous passion and intimacy to develop. However, if you are excited about developing financial plans and preparing for your retirement, this Moon will be exhilarating.

Setting a structure in place to build upon later will be worthwhile. Work out the details of the addition to the house or design this year's garden. Any activity in or around the home that adds value promotes security.

Be careful with emotional encounters. Your unusual sense of detachment may not leave the best first impression. The grounding nature of this Moon will make it difficult to intuitively connect with others; therefore, it is easier to mistake desires for instinctual messages.

Pisces Moon Personality in the Aquarius Moon

This Air Moon will heighten your mental abilities and leave you incapable of emotional communication. You will draw attention to yourself with mental agility and conversational prowess. You will not have any trouble with socializing at a party. You can easily move from conversation to conversation, but don't expect to make any deep emotional connections. Aquarian emotions are well cloaked and only a select few ever get a glimpse. This doesn't mean you have to give in, just be aware of the difficulty others will have seeing your true self.

You may have difficulty in looking at your true inner-self as well. The Aquarius Moon excels at hiding emotions from the world but it's best at hiding them from you. This can be difficult since you are not used to being severed from your emotions.

Use this period of emotional detachment to your advantage. A difficult situation can be approached with relative safety. This is especially useful when your previous tools have been procrastination and avoidance.

This doesn't mean you will be free of emotion. There will ample opportunity to get in touch with your feelings. This Moon will help you set them aside for now. The emotions you ignore will arise again during the Pisces Moon.

Pisces Moon Personality in the Pisces Moon

Your natal Water Moon will make you feel as though your emotions are back to "normal." Your intuition is working well and your emotions are running smoothly. Give yourself an emotional checkup.

Make time for your partner. The Pisces Moon is the perfect time for romance. It is an ideal time for intimate moments, such as cuddling by a fire or talking quietly under the full Moon. Should you take a trip, don't worry about finances. This Moon doesn't naturally emphasize the material world. After all, romance is always more fun than practicality.

Since practical matters may be out of reach for the next few days, focus on intuition. There will be many things you just "know." It is not necessary to explain the source of this knowledge, just trust it. Be aware, be receptive to psychic impressions, and be honest enough with yourself to discern the difference between instinct and desire.

Chapter 6

The Key to Happiness

The intensity of the Moon's influence on us varies. The Moon's phase determines the strength of its involvement in our lives, while the twelve signs of the Zodiac determine its breadth.

For our purposes, the three Moon phases are the waxing Moon, the waning Moon, and the dark Moon. The twelve void of course Moons will also be discussed as a whole. Use the information in this chapter as a guide to develop energetic solutions to the effects of each Moon.

Waxing Moon

The new Moon is a time to acknowledge the beginnings in life. Starting an activity at the new Moon and sticking with it through the full Moon can create a lifelong practice of using the Moon's growing energy.

A friend of mine successfully created the habit of exercise by using the Moon's waxing energy to assist her. Rather than diet, she chose to start new eating habits by buying healthy foods. As a result, she was able to lose and maintain her weight.

The positive, growing energies of the waxing Moon are particularly conducive to improvements, repairs, and growth. The Moon's transformation from a silvery sliver to a full, shining orb reminds us of our own growth and desire to improve.

Hundreds of activities coincide with the waxing Moon's energies. Use the following examples to identify appropriate activities: initiate or continue an exercise program; paint the house; repair the car; balance the checkbook; shop for a major purchase such as a car; plan a vacation; leave on an active, fun-filled vacation; host a party; work on a major relationship; experiment with new things, ideas, or recipes; read a favorite book; participate in hobbies; be creative and artistic; ask someone on a date for the first time; write a book; select a pet; or try to become pregnant.

As you can see, the general theme of the waxing Moon is birth and growth—the beginning of new exciting experiences and the continuation of things previously begun.

Waning Moon

Just as the new Moon is a time for beginnings, the full Moon is a time for endings. As the Moon changes from full to dark, its effect on nature shifts, changing from a growing, progressive force to a dying, retreating force. To have help in giving up a bad habit or bringing a project to a close, start the process on the full Moon and progress towards completion as the Moon wanes.

While adding exercise and a proper diet to her life, my friend also gave up smoking. She stopped smoking on the full Moon and allowed her urges to die as the Moon waned.

It is best to align tasks which require a decreasing or letting go with the waning Moon. The waning Moon, which begins as the full Moon, decreases to a sliver just before it disappears completely. It is a shining portrayal of the decline seen in the death process.

Again, hundreds of activities naturally align themselves with the declining energies of the waning Moon, including the following activities: start or continue a diet; clean the house; hold a garage sale; cut the grass; harvest garden crops; turn under old garden growth for the winter; write a last will and testament; sell a car, or a house, or anything else of value; quit a job; visit a stylist for a haircut; clean out closets; give up smoking or drinking; reduce stress; or pay bills.

Any activity which requires a decline or death of any nature is well suited to the waning Moon. When we break an old habit, we kill it. Once it is dead and gone, there is space for something new. It is common to develop a new habit when giving up an old one. A void is left by the things we give up. It's equally beneficial, and very efficient, to replace an old bad habit with a new good one, thereby filling the void. Push out an old bad habit in the waning Moon by starting something wonderful in the waxing Moon.

Dark Moon

The few days between the last sliver of the waning Moon and the first sliver of the waxing Moon is known as the dark Moon. It signals a time for regeneration and renewal. The darkness is a reminder that all life must die.

Death is common to all things. Every activity, job, or thing dies at the end of its cycle. The process of reading a book dies when the book is finished; a job dies when you leave it; and objects die when they are used or broken. I have mourned finishing a good book, as I have mourned quitting a job.

After two weeks of concentrated effort directed at ending something, take the opportunity to mourn that which has died and recover from its loss. The dark Moon is a time to look inward. Assess what happened and how the situation was handled.

A fellow firewalker offered sound advice. When an important aspect of life ends, give it a funeral service. Experience its death. After receiving an impersonal wedding announcement from a past lover, my friend took a memento of her relationship with him to the beach. She meditated with it, said good-bye to her old relationship and tossed the memento into the ocean.

A death ritual provides the opportunity to release that which has ended and beginning the mourning process. This is useful following the death of anything, but especially when ending relationships. The willingness to allow the relationship to die begets mourning and healing.

Void of Course Moon

This phase of the Moon's regular cycle is not conducive to anything productive or beneficial except play and relaxation. Since the Moon's energies are not being "filtered" through one of the twelve Zodiac positions its energies are random and, therefore, useless. The best course of action in a void of course Moon is to avoid commitments, intense situations, and the need to make decisions. If decisions are necessary, the next best choice is to follow a previously set course. The void of course Moon typically doesn't last more than a few hours and should not be more than a nuisance.

There are twelve void of course Moons, but we will treat them as if they were one. The difference in their effects on us is negligible. The void of course Moons act as a space between the Moon signs, in which the Moon's energies are random and unpredictable. Often the void of course Moon will take on the characteristics of the coming Moon sign before the Moon actually enters that sign.

It is important to match lunar energies to the task. When the Moon is waxing, the tasks at hand should be those that require new and increasing energy. Objectives that require a decrease in size or energy are best left to the waning Moon.

Of course, it is possible to get things accomplished that are not in synchronicity with the Moon's phases; however, changes are more easily accomplished in concert with the Moon's energies rather than in conflict with them.

The Moons of the Zodiac

The twelve signs of the Zodiac are unique in their characteristics and influence. When the Moon passes through the signs it takes on the energies of each sign, which in turn affects personalities and emotions. Since everyone's makeup is different, the effect of a particular Moon will vary.

What to Do in an Aries Moon

Start new projects which can be completed quickly. Activities begun in this Moon do not have much staying power and will usually be abandoned in the near future. Volunteer some time to local environmental groups. They will appreciate your help and be motivated by your fresh enthusiasm.

Try out new recipes if they require cooking or baking. Save cold meals for another time. Dehydrate fruits for the coming winter. This is a good time to lose a small amount of weight very quickly, but don't plan on it being a permanent loss. Exercise, exercise, and exercise—all of this Fire energy should be used for something.

Collect old debts as long as they're not from friends. Collection efforts in this Moon will be forceful, possibly harsh. Property and stock market speculation are appropriate right now. Don't make any long-term purchases.

Take on a small project like a new set of shelves for the garage. Build a new entertainment center from a kit. Try surfing the Internet. Cultivate the garden. This Moon will help to eliminate weeds and pests.

What to Do in a Taurus Moon

This is the best Moon to begin projects which cannot be completed quickly. It's also the best time to form lifelong habits (hopefully good ones). A new activity will become habitual and very difficult to change.

This is great Moon for enhancing your appearance. Buy some new clothes, or straighten your teeth. Choose a new hairstyle and relax with a massage and facial.

Food becomes of major importance in this Earth Moon. Rather than succumb to gluttony, try to focus on cooking. Prepare a great family dinner. Keep cooking until the eating urge passes. Cook for the next couple of days if need be.

Open a savings account, or buy a house and move. Start to work on a financial plan devised during the Capricorn Moon. Buy a new car or repair an old one.

Volunteer for fundraising at a local charity. They always need help. Call on business contacts. Take on new responsibilities at work or start a new job. Make a new effort in getting to work on time. Train a new employee, or for that matter, train a pet.

Begin a construction project. Remodel the garage and paint the kids' bedrooms. Add that deck and jacuzzi off the back porch. Organize and plan the garden. Plant root crops and leafy vegetables. If nothing else sounds exciting, read a book.

What to Do in a Gemini Moon

Other people's opinions will have a great impact in this Moon. A new project will have some staying power but will probably not complete as planned. This kind of energy is very conducive to writing as an art form.

Break old habits. Eliminate them now and be done with them by the next Scorpio Moon. Weed the garden. (Don't let those noxious growths get a foothold.)

This is a good time to fill the social calendar. Go to parties and have some fun. Check out the local singles club or join a gym. Take a class at the community college or travel with a group. Look into "save the earth" organizations. Check out the latest generation of games on CD-ROM—they will steal several hours in a single sitting.

What to Do in a Cancer Moon

Use intuition when developing a good rapport with others. It will help you to understand their needs and know how to serve them.

Bake bread or cookies. Gain some weight. Try canning apricots. I enjoy making mead and often begin the process in the Cancer Moon. Invite friends over for some down-home family cooking: soups and stews, homemade bread, and baked Alaska for dessert.

Any activity around the home that beautifies or enhances domesticity is appropriate. New furniture may be in order—add an antique to the collection.

This is good opportunity to change outward appearance. Change your hair color or get a perm. Help to beautify the neighborhood. Pick up the cans and bottles discarded along the streets or in the nearby park, and don't forget to recycle.

Collecting money from friends will be much easier right now. Concern for their well-being will come through. They will feel obligated to pay you back.

The garden is a priority. There is no better time to plant and water. Studies show planting in this Moon produces healthier and more fruitful plants.

What to Do in a Leo Moon

Concentrate on work with charities or any institutional program. The development of an idea that will spawn a whole new process for you is a perfect activity for this Moon. Magnanimous behavior will satisfy the craving to be recognized. Volunteer time to youth groups.

Paint the exterior of the house. To gain attention paint it a very bright color. Install a security fence around the property. Consider buying an expensive car to park in front of the newly secured and painted house. Move to a new neighborhood. If all else fails, throw a party. It will provide a stage in front of a captive audience.

Use the extra energy of this Fire Moon to exercise and lose some weight. Cook with foods that encourage the body's metabolism. Dry fruits and vegetables rather than throwing out the extras. If cooking is bothersome, visit the most elegant restaurant in town. It is time to pull weeds again. The first weeds to come up are the trendsetters. If they are killed organically, very few weeds will follow.

What to Do in a Virgo Moon

This Moon is conducive to completing any detailed activity. I found that editing my book was a perfect activity for this Moon. It may be satisfying to complete a crossword puzzle or compete in a chess tournament. Clean out your car.

Avoid activities that depend on initiative and global problem-solving abilities. Any task at work requiring detailed analysis will be easily accomplished, as will additional work delegated by the boss. Take on new job responsibilities.

Enroll in a technical institute to learn a new job skill or begin to study a foreign language. Join the local astrology club, or take cooking lessons. The local zoo or humane society needs volunteers for a variety of tasks—check into it.

A weight-loss program built around eating natural foods with just the right amount of sodium and fat will be a resounding success. Study those labels and buy healthy food.

What to Do in a Libra Moon

Join a social group or participate in social functions. This Moon breeds positive interactions with others. Talk about yourself. Don't worry, this will only develop intimacy. Attend some parties or host one. Any work requiring salesmanship will be productive. Volunteer at a charity or children's hospital.

Cook for another—make some muffins and take them to work. No one ever complains about more food around the workplace. A romantic candlelit dinner for two could go a long way in a relationship.

Update the wardrobe. Try a new hairstyle. Give some thought to contact lenses or change your frame style. Consider facial hair. A beard, moustache, or goatee might do the trick.

Vine plants are best sown in this Moon. The roots will be stronger and healthier.

What to Do in a Scorpio Moon

Maximize psychic abilities. This will help you to deal with strangers and to make major decisions, such as buying a car. Trust your instincts. Plan a lustfully romantic evening or weekend away. Shop for sexy underwear or clothes.

Bulk up for football or hockey tryouts. This is another good Moon for brewing beer. Making jellies and candies feels good. I have never met a Scorpio Sun or Scorpio Moon that didn't like antiques. Buy one, but not as a gift.

This is good time to end things, especially relationships. The end will be swift and permanent. Avoid chopping down a tree in this Moon, because it will not grow back. Expend some energy helping a conservation group.

The Scorpio Moon is a Water Moon and like all Water Moons, it's well suited for healing. Buy herbal medicines. Harvesting herbs should be done later, but planting them is appropriate. In fact, planting in general is a good idea.

What to Do in a Sagittarius Moon

This Moon encourages faith in life and spirit. Faith can be used to help accomplish difficult tasks such as changing jobs. Use your imagination when deciding on a career path or vacation plans.

Rest and recreation are perfectly suited to the Sagittarius Moon. Give in to spontaneity. Have faith and trust that everything will work out.

Speaking of faith, a church or religious organization needs your help. Don't just contribute money—give them your time.

The last of the Fire Moons should include traveling. Avoid a planned group trip—just go. If you are a little short of cash for the trip, ask for a loan. Don't forget to send postcards. Eat, drink, and overindulge. Be careless, it's all right—this is a vacation. Don't forget to pack the aspirin and antacid.

After every planting Moon comes a weeding Moon. Fire Moons are not nurturing. Weed your garden.

What to Do in a Capricorn Moon

The Capricorn Moon is well suited for structured plans. Plans made will develop with strength on a well-laid foundation, especially if there is a personal financial interest.

Set financial goals and plan for the future. Balance the checkbook and work out payment terms with creditors or on new purchases. Investments will be sound right now in stocks, bonds, rentals houses, antiques, artwork, and real estate.

Take a look at the temperature of your water heater—turn it down to conserve resources. Lights are often left on when not in use. Make an effort to turn them off and save money on the electric bill.

Develop the company softball team roster for next season or plan a week's vacation. Set up a regular maintenance schedule for the car and open a savings account that automatically deposits your paycheck in your account.

The smell of baking permeates a home and adds wonderful appeal. Why not bake a pie for dessert this evening? This is a great Moon to plan or start a diet.

Plant root crops that didn't get planted in the Taurus Moon. Potatoes flourish in the Capricorn Moon.

What to Do in an Aquarius Moon

This is the Moon for chemically treating hair. Work on the winter tan in the tanning salon and get a manicure. A diet will be effective with the help of a weight-loss business. An attempt to lose weight without the encouragement and assistance of others should be saved for another Moon.

Resist old cravings as long as possible, then give in. Since we're talking about food, this would be a good time to can preserves.

"Neither a borrower or a lender be," but it may be the right time to borrow money from an institution. Avoid lending money. Negotiate terms for a new car or home improvements. Ask for a discount at the grocery store.

Social events are a priority right now. Host a party at your place or join a social group. Traveling in groups will enhance the trip. Hang out with friends.

Write to senators and congressmen about environmental concerns. Make sure they understand what's expected of them.

Projects around the house should be limited to painting, wallpapering, carpeting or tiling a floor. Change only the outward appearance. Avoid structural work.

Kill those weeds. Dig them out and burn them.

What to Do in a Pisces Moon

The Pisces Moon is a time for recuperation, reorganization, and planning on the heels of a completed project or one that went sour. Regroup and plan the next attack.

Use this Water Moon to help the watery portions of our planet. Donate time and money to an environmental cause or help clean up a beach.

Organize a filing cabinet or self-storage locker. It is time for spring cleaning. Go through a closet and give to charity all of the clothes not worn at least once last year.

The Pisces Moon is the most romantic. A wedding or honeymoon would be perfect. If that's too serious, try a weekend at the beach. Get lost in a romance.

Like the other two Water Moons, canning foods and brewing beer are well worth the time. Cook foods that need to age. Chili and spaghetti sauce always taste better the next day.

Mail important packages if they must arrive on time. Remember to insure them. It is time to nurture the garden. Water the plants and speak softly to them. This is a time for growth.

Self-awareness is the key to using the Moon. Continue to write in the journal. Create a safe space to feel and express emotions. Consider these emotions when making choices. When timing is not an issue, include the Moon as one of the factors in making that choice. For example, plan on avoiding the Cancer Moon when doing anything that will test the security of the home space. Don't inadvertently plan a garage sale on a Cancer Moon. We often feel more secure when we have our possessions around us, and by selling it we are testing that sense of security. The Cancer Moon is also a sentimental one and selling things owned for years will be difficult. A more positive approach to the Cancer Moon might be to work on home improvement projects or spend some time just enjoying the home space. Remember, it's only a matter of choice.

There may be as many different beliefs as to how we should live our lives as there are people on the earth. Most people will say they want to live happily ever after but are usually not doing so. Some are not happy because they are unwilling to be and others possibly don't know how. Most people have not learned that happiness is a choice they make every day, and often several times a day.

Those unwilling to live happily often feel the way they do because they are comfortable. Not that people wish to be unhappy—they have simply compromised many of their desires and standards to fit in the mold of society. They no longer think complete happiness is possible. They have responsibilities; therefore, are satisfied to say that life is "good enough." It's what they know and deciding to be happy would require a change in their life and possibly a risk. They might get what they want, or they might fail, both of which can be very scary concepts.

Happiness has nothing to do with the difficulties we encounter as we make our way in this world. Happiness is nothing more than a state of mind. Actually "happy" is defined in the dictionary as "contented of mind." With this definition in mind, happiness can be increased by simply reducing the worries and stresses which weigh heavily on each of us. This can be done in part as previously suggested: take advantage of the Moon; be responsible, don't be a victim; fix the problem, not the blame; and listen. Happiness is found in being at ease with your environment, and being at peace with yourself.

Practice these concepts. With practice they will become natural. Tune in to the Moon and understand its changes. This attunement will foster self-awareness and in turn will open us to the feelings of others. Fully participating in a relationship means sharing our feelings with another and providing safe space for them to share with us. Over time, this leads to fewer emotional ups and downs, and a richer, more complete life experience. Choose to be happy.

PRAYER

Great Spirit, known to us by many names,
it is from you, all life is born
and to you, all life must return.

With your wisdom we travel our path,
through your patience we learn our lessons,
and with your nurturing we grow.

By coming to know ourselves may we come to know you,
by learning to care for ourselves may we learn to care for you,
by bringing health to ourselves may we heal you.

Great Spirit, known to us by many names,
walk with us by day and dream with us by night.
Go in peace and blessed be.

Appendix

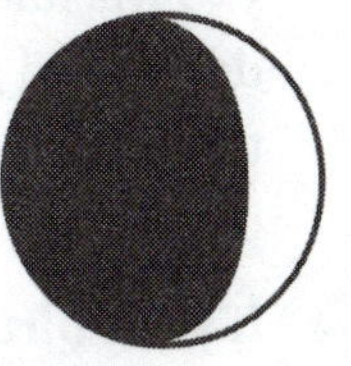

Lunar Ephemeris

The following system for determining the Moon's position was developed by Grant Lewi. It was originally published in Lewi's *Astrology for the Millions* (Llewellyn Publications).

Grant Lewi's System

1. Find your birth year in the tables.
2. Run down the left-hand column and see if your date is there.

3. **If your date is in the left-hand column**, run over this line until you come to the column under your birth year. Here you will find a number. This is your **base number.** Write it down, and go directly to the part of the directions under the heading, "What to Do with Your Base Number" on page 192.
4. **If your birth date is not in the left-hand column**, get a pencil and paper. Your birth date falls between two numbers in the left hand column. Look at the date closest *after* your birth date, run over this line to your birth year. Write down the number you find there, and label it "top number." Having done this, write directly beneath it on your piece of paper the number printed just above it in the table. Label this "bottom number." **Subtract the bottom number from the top number. (If the top number is smaller, add 360 to it and then subtract.) The result is your difference.**
5. Go back to the left-hand column and find the date next *before* your birth date. Determine the number of days between this date and your birth date. Write this down and label it "intervening days."
6. In the **Table of Difference** below, note which group your **difference** (found at 4 above) falls in:

Difference	*Daily Motion*
80–87	12 degrees
88–94	13 degrees
95–101	14 degrees
102–106	15 degrees

Note: If you were born in a leap year and use the difference between February 26 and March 5, use the following special table:

Difference	*Daily Motion*
94–99	12 degrees
100–108	13 degrees
109–115	14 degrees
116–122	15 degrees

Write down the **daily motion** corresponding to your place in the proper **Table of Difference** above.

7. Multiply this daily motion by the number labeled **intervening days** (found at 5, above).
8. Add the result of step 7 to your bottom number (under 4). The result of this is your **base number**. If it is more than 360, subtract 360 from it and call the result your **base number**.

What to Do with Your Base Number

Turn to the **Table of Base Numbers** (page 215) and locate your **base number** in it. At the top of the column you will find the **sign** your Moon was in when you were born. At the left you will find the **degree** your Moon occupied at:

- 12 noon of your birth date if you were born under Greenwich (London) Mean Time;
- 7 A.M. of your birth date if you were born under Eastern Standard Time;
- 6 A.M. of your birth date if you were born under Central Standard Time;
- 5 A.M. of your birth date if you were born under Mountain Standard Time;
- 4 A.M. of your birth date if you were born under Pacific Standard Time.

If you don't know the hour of your birth, accept this as your Moon's sign and degree. If you do know the hour of your birth, get the exact degree as follows:

- If you were born *after* 7 A.M., Eastern Standard Time (6 A.M. Central Standard Time, etc.), determine the number of hours after this time that you were born. Divide this by two. Add this to your base number, and the result in the table will be the exact degree and sign of the Moon on the year, month, date, and hour of your birth.
- If you were born *before* 7 a.m. EST (6 a.m. CST, etc.), determine the number of hours before that time that you were born. Divide this by two. Subtract this from your base number, and the result in the table will be the exact degree and sign of the Moon on the year, month, date, and hour of your birth.

The Moon Through the Signs

	1901	1902	1903	1904	1905	1906	1907	1908	1909	1910
Jan. 1	55	188	308	76	227	358	119	246	39	168
Jan. 8	149	272	37	179	319	82	208	350	129	252
Jan. 15	234	2	141	270	43	174	311	81	213	346
Jan. 22	327	101	234	353	138	273	44	164	309	84
Jan. 29	66	196	317	84	238	6	128	255	50	175
Feb. 5	158	280	46	188	328	90	219	359	138	259
Feb. 12	241	12	149	279	51	184	319	90	221	356
Feb. 19	335	111	242	2	146	283	52	173	317	94
Feb. 26	76	204	326	92	248	13	136	264	60	184
Mar. 5	166	288	57	211	336	98	229	21	147	267
Mar. 12	249	22	157	300	60	194	328	110	230	5
Mar. 19	344	121	250	24	154	293	60	195	325	105
Mar. 26	86	212	334	116	258	22	144	288	69	192
Apr. 2	175	296	68	219	345	106	240	29	155	276
Apr. 9	258	31	167	309	69	202	338	118	240	13
Apr. 16	352	132	258	33	163	304	68	204	334	115
Apr. 23	96	220	342	127	267	31	152	299	77	201
Apr. 30	184	304	78	227	354	114	250	38	164	285
May 7	267	40	177	317	78	210	348	126	249	21
May 14	1	142	266	42	172	313	76	212	344	124
May 21	104	229	350	138	275	40	160	310	85	210
May 28	193	313	87	236	2	123	259	47	172	294
June 4	277	48	187	324	88	219	358	134	258	30
June 11	11	151	275	50	182	322	85	220	355	132
June 18	112	238	359	149	283	48	169	320	93	218
June 25	201	322	96	245	11	133	267	57	180	304
July 2	286	57	197	333	97	228	8	142	267	40
July 9	21	160	283	58	193	330	94	228	6	140
July 16	121	247	7	159	291	57	178	330	102	226
July 23	209	332	105	255	18	143	276	66	188	314
July 30	295	66	206	341	105	239	17	151	275	51
Aug. 6	32	168	292	66	204	338	103	237	17	148
Aug. 13	130	255	17	168	301	65	188	339	111	234
Aug. 20	217	341	113	265	27	152	285	76	197	323
Aug. 27	303	77	215	350	113	250	25	160	283	62
Sept. 3	43	176	301	75	215	346	111	246	27	157

	1901	1902	1903	1904	1905	1906	1907	1908	1909	1910
Sept. 10	139	263	27	176	310	73	198	347	121	242
Sept. 17	225	350	123	274	35	161	294	85	205	331
Sept. 24	311	88	223	358	122	261	33	169	292	73
Oct. 1	53	185	309	85	224	355	119	256	35	166
Oct. 8	149	271	36	185	320	81	207	356	130	250
Oct. 15	233	359	133	283	44	169	305	93	214	339
Oct. 22	319	99	231	7	130	271	42	177	301	83
Oct. 29	62	194	317	95	233	5	127	266	44	176
Nov. 5	158	279	45	193	329	89	216	5	139	259
Nov. 12	242	6	144	291	53	177	316	101	223	347
Nov. 19	328	109	239	15	140	280	50	185	311	91
Nov. 26	70	203	325	105	241	14	135	276	52	185
Dec. 3	168	288	54	203	338	98	224	15	148	268
Dec. 10	251	14	155	299	61	185	327	109	231	356
Dec. 17	338	118	248	23	150	289	59	193	322	99
Dec. 24	78	213	333	115	249	23	143	286	61	194
Dec. 31	176	296	61	213	346	107	232	26	155	277

	1911	1912	1913	1914	1915	1916	1917	1918	1919	1920
Jan. 1	289	57	211	337	100	228	23	147	270	39
Jan. 8	20	162	299	61	192	332	110	231	5	143
Jan. 15	122	251	23	158	293	61	193	329	103	231
Jan. 22	214	335	120	256	23	145	290	68	193	316
Jan. 29	298	66	221	345	108	237	32	155	278	49
Feb. 5	31	170	308	69	203	340	118	239	16	150
Feb. 12	130	260	32	167	302	70	203	338	113	239
Feb. 19	222	344	128	266	31	154	298	78	201	325
Feb. 26	306	75	231	353	116	248	41	164	286	60
Mar. 5	42	192	317	77	214	2	127	248	26	172
Mar. 12	140	280	41	176	311	89	212	346	123	259
Mar. 19	230	5	136	276	39	176	308	87	209	346
Mar. 26	314	100	239	2	124	273	49	173	294	85
Apr. 2	52	200	326	86	223	10	135	257	35	181
Apr. 9	150	288	51	184	321	97	222	355	133	267
Apr. 16	238	14	146	286	48	184	318	96	218	355
Apr. 23	322	111	247	11	132	284	57	181	303	96
Apr. 30	61	208	334	96	232	19	143	267	43	190
May 7	160	296	60	192	331	105	231	4	142	275

	1911	1912	1913	1914	1915	1916	1917	1918	1919	1920
May 14	246	22	156	294	56	192	329	104	227	3
May 21	331	122	255	20	141	294	66	190	312	105
May 28	69	218	342	106	240	29	151	277	51	200
June 4	170	304	69	202	341	114	240	14	151	284
June 11	255	30	167	302	65	200	340	112	235	11
June 18	340	132	264	28	151	304	74	198	322	114
June 25	78	228	350	115	249	39	159	286	60	209
July 2	179	312	78	212	349	122	248	25	159	293
July 9	264	39	178	310	74	209	350	120	244	20
July 16	349	141	273	36	161	312	84	206	332	123
July 23	87	237	358	125	258	48	168	295	70	218
July 30	187	321	86	223	357	131	256	36	167	302
Aug. 6	272	48	188	319	82	219	360	129	252	31
Aug. 13	359	150	282	44	171	320	93	214	342	131
Aug. 20	96	246	6	133	268	57	177	303	81	226
Aug. 27	195	330	94	234	5	140	265	46	175	310
Sept. 3	281	57	198	328	90	229	9	138	260	41
Sept. 10	9	158	292	52	180	329	102	222	351	140
Sept. 17	107	255	15	141	279	65	186	312	91	234
Sept. 24	203	339	103	244	13	149	274	56	184	319
Oct. 1	288	68	206	337	98	240	17	148	268	52
Oct. 8	18	167	301	61	189	338	111	231	360	150
Oct. 15	118	263	24	149	290	73	195	320	102	242
Oct. 22	212	347	113	254	22	157	284	65	193	326
Oct. 29	296	78	214	346	106	250	25	157	276	61
Nov. 5	26	177	309	70	197	348	119	240	7	161
Nov. 12	129	271	33	158	300	81	203	329	112	250
Nov. 19	221	355	123	262	31	164	295	73	202	334
Nov. 26	305	88	223	355	115	259	34	165	285	70
Dec. 3	34	187	317	79	205	359	127	249	16	171
Dec. 10	138	279	41	168	310	89	211	340	120	259
Dec. 17	230	3	134	270	40	172	305	81	211	343
Dec. 24	313	97	232	3	124	267	44	173	294	78
Dec. 31	42	198	325	87	214	9	135	257	25	181

	1921	1922	1923	1924	1925	1926	1927	1928	1929	1930
Jan. 1	194	317	80	211	5	127	250	23	176	297
Jan. 8	280	41	177	313	90	211	349	123	260	22

	1921	1922	1923	1924	1925	1926	1927	1928	1929	1930
Jan. 15	4	141	275	41	175	312	86	211	346	123
Jan. 22	101	239	3	127	272	51	172	297	83	222
Jan. 29	203	325	88	222	13	135	258	34	184	306
Feb. 5	289	49	188	321	99	220	359	131	269	31
Feb. 12	14	149	284	49	185	320	95	219	356	131
Feb. 19	110	249	11	135	281	60	181	305	93	230
Feb. 26	211	334	96	233	21	144	266	45	191	314
Mar. 5	297	58	197	343	107	230	8	153	276	41
Mar. 12	23	157	294	69	194	328	105	238	6	140
Mar. 19	119	258	19	157	292	68	190	327	104	238
Mar. 26	219	343	104	258	29	153	275	70	200	323
Apr. 2	305	68	205	352	115	240	16	163	284	51
Apr. 9	33	166	304	77	204	337	114	247	14	149
Apr. 16	130	266	28	164	303	76	198	335	115	246
Apr. 23	227	351	114	268	38	161	285	79	208	331
Apr. 30	313	78	214	1	123	250	25	172	292	61
May 7	42	176	313	85	212	348	123	256	23	160
May 14	141	274	37	173	314	84	207	344	125	254
May 21	236	359	123	277	47	169	295	88	217	339
May 28	321	88	222	11	131	259	34	181	301	70
June 4	50	186	321	94	220	358	131	264	31	171
June 11	152	282	45	182	324	93	215	354	135	263
June 18	245	7	134	285	56	177	305	96	226	347
June 25	330	97	232	20	139	268	44	190	310	78
July 2	58	197	329	103	229	9	139	273	40	181
July 9	162	291	54	192	333	101	223	4	144	272
July 16	254	15	144	294	65	185	315	104	236	355
July 23	338	106	242	28	148	276	54	198	319	87
July 30	67	208	337	112	238	20	147	282	49	191
Aug. 6	171	300	62	202	341	110	231	15	152	281
Aug. 13	264	24	153	302	74	194	324	114	244	4
Aug. 20	347	114	253	36	157	285	65	206	328	95
Aug. 27	76	218	346	120	248	29	156	290	59	200
Sept. 3	179	309	70	213	350	119	239	25	161	290
Sept. 10	273	32	162	312	83	203	332	124	252	13
Sept. 17	356	122	264	44	166	293	75	214	337	105
Sept. 24	86	227	354	128	258	38	165	298	70	208
Oct. 1	187	318	78	223	358	128	248	35	169	298

	1921	1922	1923	1924	1925	1926	1927	1928	1929	1930
Oct. 8	281	41	170	322	91	212	340	134	260	23
Oct. 15	5	132	274	52	175	303	85	222	345	115
Oct. 22	97	235	3	136	269	46	174	306	81	216
Oct. 29	196	327	87	232	7	137	257	44	179	307
Nov. 5	289	50	178	332	99	221	349	144	268	31
Nov. 12	13	142	283	61	183	313	93	231	353	126
Nov. 19	107	243	12	144	279	54	183	315	91	225
Nov. 26	206	335	96	241	17	145	266	52	189	314
Dec. 3	297	59	187	343	107	230	359	154	276	39
Dec. 10	21	152	291	70	191	324	101	240	1	137
Dec. 17	117	252	21	153	289	63	191	324	99	234
Dec. 24	216	343	105	249	28	152	275	60	199	322
Dec. 31	305	67	197	352	115	237	9	162	285	47

	1931	1932	1933	1934	1935	1936	1937	1938	1939	1940
Jan. 1	60	196	346	107	231	8	156	277	41	181
Jan. 8	162	294	70	193	333	104	240	4	144	275
Jan. 15	257	20	158	294	68	190	329	104	239	360
Jan. 22	342	108	255	32	152	278	67	202	323	88
Jan. 29	68	207	353	116	239	19	163	286	49	191
Feb. 5	171	302	78	203	342	113	248	14	153	284
Feb. 12	267	28	168	302	78	198	339	113	248	8
Feb. 19	351	116	266	40	161	286	78	210	332	96
Feb. 26	77	217	1	124	248	29	171	294	59	200
Mar. 5	179	324	86	213	350	135	256	25	161	306
Mar. 12	276	48	176	311	86	218	347	123	256	29
Mar. 19	360	137	277	48	170	308	89	218	340	119
Mar. 26	86	241	10	132	258	52	180	302	69	223
Apr. 2	187	334	94	223	358	144	264	34	169	315
Apr. 9	285	57	185	321	95	227	355	133	264	38
Apr. 16	9	146	287	56	178	317	99	226	349	128
Apr. 23	96	250	18	140	268	61	189	310	80	231
Apr. 30	196	343	102	232	7	153	273	43	179	323
May 7	293	66	193	332	103	237	4	144	272	47
May 14	17	155	297	64	187	327	108	235	357	139
May 21	107	258	28	148	278	69	198	318	90	239
May 28	205	351	111	241	17	161	282	51	189	331
June 4	301	75	201	343	111	245	13	154	280	55

	1931	**1932**	**1933**	**1934**	**1935**	**1936**	**1937**	**1938**	**1939**	**1940**
June 11	25	165	306	73	195	337	117	244	5	150
June 18	117	267	37	157	288	78	207	327	99	248
June 25	215	360	120	249	28	169	291	60	200	339
July 2	309	84	211	353	119	254	23	164	289	64
July 9	33	176	315	82	203	348	125	253	13	160
July 16	126	276	46	165	297	87	216	336	108	258
July 23	226	8	130	258	38	177	300	69	210	347
July 30	317	92	221	2	128	262	33	173	298	72
Aug. 6	41	187	323	91	211	359	133	261	21	170
Aug. 13	135	285	54	175	305	97	224	346	116	268
Aug. 20	237	16	138	267	49	185	308	78	220	355
Aug. 27	326	100	232	10	136	270	44	181	307	80
Sept. 3	49	197	331	100	220	8	142	270	31	179
Sept. 10	143	295	62	184	314	107	232	355	125	278
Sept. 17	247	24	147	277	58	194	317	89	228	4
Sept. 24	335	108	243	18	145	278	55	189	316	88
Oct. 1	58	206	341	108	229	17	152	278	40	188
Oct. 8	151	306	70	193	322	117	240	4	134	288
Oct. 15	256	32	155	287	66	203	324	100	236	13
Oct. 22	344	116	253	27	154	287	64	198	324	98
Oct. 29	68	214	350	116	239	25	162	286	49	196
Nov. 5	161	316	78	201	332	126	248	12	145	297
Nov. 12	264	41	162	298	74	212	333	111	244	22
Nov. 19	353	125	262	36	162	296	73	207	332	108
Nov. 26	77	222	0	124	248	33	172	294	58	205
Dec. 3	171	325	87	209	343	135	257	19	156	305
Dec. 10	272	50	171	309	82	220	341	120	253	30
Dec. 17	1	135	271	45	170	306	81	217	340	118
Dec. 24	86	231	10	132	256	43	181	302	66	214
Dec. 31	182	333	95	217	354	142	265	27	167	313

	1941	**1942**	**1943**	**194**	**1945**	**1946**	**1947**	**1948**	**1949**	**1950**
Jan. 1	325	88	211	353	135	258	22	165	305	68
Jan. 8	50	176	315	85	219	348	126	256	29	160
Jan. 15	141	276	50	169	312	87	220	340	123	258
Jan. 22	239	12	133	258	52	182	303	69	224	352
Jan. 29	333	96	221	2	143	266	32	174	314	75
Feb. 5	57	186	323	95	227	358	134	265	37	170

	1941	**1942**	**1943**	**1944**	**1945**	**1946**	**1947**	**1948**	**1949**	**1950**
Feb. 12	150	285	58	178	320	96	228	349	131	268
Feb. 19	250	20	142	267	62	190	312	78	234	359
Feb. 26	342	104	231	11	152	274	43	182	323	83
Mar. 5	65	196	331	116	236	8	142	286	46	179
Mar. 12	158	295	66	199	328	107	236	10	139	279
Mar. 19	261	28	150	290	72	198	320	102	243	8
Mar. 26	351	112	242	34	161	281	53	204	332	91
Apr. 2	74	205	340	125	244	16	152	294	55	187
Apr. 9	166	306	74	208	337	117	244	19	148	289
Apr. 16	270	36	158	300	81	206	328	112	252	17
Apr. 23	360	120	252	42	170	290	63	212	340	100
Apr. 30	83	214	350	133	254	25	162	302	64	195
May 7	174	316	82	217	346	127	252	27	158	299
May 14	279	45	166	311	90	215	336	123	260	26
May 21	9	128	261	50	179	299	72	221	349	110
May 28	92	222	1	141	263	33	173	310	73	204
June 4	184	326	91	226	356	137	261	36	168	307
June 11	287	54	174	322	98	224	344	134	268	34
June 18	17	137	270	60	187	308	81	231	357	119
June 25	102	231	11	149	272	42	183	318	82	213
July 2	194	335	99	234	7	145	269	44	179	316
July 9	296	63	183	332	106	233	353	144	277	43
July 16	25	147	279	70	195	318	89	241	5	129
July 23	110	240	21	157	280	52	192	327	91	224
July 30	205	343	108	242	18	153	278	52	190	324
Aug. 6	304	71	192	341	115	241	3	153	286	51
Aug. 13	33	156	287	80	203	327	98	251	13	138
Aug. 20	119	250	30	165	289	63	201	336	99	235
Aug. 27	216	351	117	250	28	162	287	61	200	332
Sept. 3	314	80	201	350	125	249	13	161	296	59
Sept. 10	41	165	296	90	211	336	108	260	21	146
Sept. 17	127	261	39	174	297	74	209	345	107	246
Sept. 24	226	359	126	259	38	170	295	70	209	341
Oct. 1	323	88	211	358	135	257	22	170	306	67
Oct. 8	49	174	306	99	220	344	118	269	30	154
Oct. 15	135	272	47	183	305	84	217	353	116	256
Oct. 22	236	8	134	269	47	180	303	80	217	351
Oct. 29	333	95	220	7	144	265	31	179	315	75

	1941	1942	1943	1944	1945	1946	1947	1948	1949	1950
Nov. 5	58	181	317	107	229	352	129	277	39	162
Nov. 12	143	283	55	192	314	94	225	1	125	265
Nov. 19	244	18	141	279	55	189	311	90	225	0
Nov. 26	343	104	229	16	153	274	39	189	323	84
Dec. 3	67	189	328	115	237	360	140	284	47	171
Dec. 10	153	292	64	200	324	103	234	9	136	274
Dec. 17	252	28	149	289	63	199	319	100	234	9
Dec. 24	351	112	237	27	161	282	47	199	331	93
Dec. 31	76	198	338	123	246	9	150	293	55	180

	1951	1952	1953	1954	1955	1956	1957	1958	1959	1960
Jan. 1	194	336	115	238	6	147	285	47	178	317
Jan. 8	297	67	199	331	107	237	9	143	278	47
Jan. 15	30	150	294	70	200	320	104	242	9	131
Jan. 22	114	240	35	161	284	51	207	331	94	223
Jan. 29	204	344	124	245	17	155	294	55	189	325
Feb. 5	305	76	207	341	116	246	18	152	287	56
Feb. 12	38	159	302	80	208	330	112	252	17	140
Feb. 19	122	249	45	169	292	61	216	340	102	233
Feb. 26	215	352	133	253	27	163	303	63	199	333
Mar. 5	314	96	216	350	125	266	27	161	297	75
Mar. 12	46	180	310	91	216	351	121	262	25	161
Mar. 19	130	274	54	178	300	86	224	349	110	259
Mar. 26	225	14	142	262	37	185	312	72	208	356
Apr. 2	324	104	226	358	135	274	37	169	307	83
Apr. 9	54	189	319	100	224	360	131	271	34	170
Apr. 16	138	285	62	187	308	97	232	357	118	269
Apr. 23	235	23	150	271	46	194	320	82	217	5
Apr. 30	334	112	235	6	146	282	46	177	317	91
May 7	62	197	330	109	232	8	142	279	42	177
May 14	146	296	70	196	316	107	240	6	127	279
May 21	243	32	158	280	54	204	328	91	225	15
May 28	344	120	244	15	155	290	55	187	326	100
June 4	71	205	341	117	241	16	153	288	51	186
June 11	155	306	79	204	325	117	249	14	137	288
June 18	252	42	166	290	63	214	336	101	234	25
June 25	354	128	253	26	164	298	63	198	335	109
July 2	80	214	351	125	250	24	164	296	60	195

	1951	1952	1953	1954	1955	1956	1957	1958	1959	1960
July 9	164	315	88	212	335	126	259	22	147	297
July 16	260	52	174	299	72	223	344	110	243	34
July 23	3	137	261	37	173	307	71	209	343	118
July 30	89	222	2	134	258	33	174	304	68	205
Aug. 6	174	324	97	220	345	134	268	30	156	305
Aug. 13	270	62	182	308	82	232	353	118	254	42
Aug. 20	11	146	269	48	181	316	79	220	351	126
Aug. 27	97	232	11	143	267	43	183	314	76	215
Sept. 3	184	332	107	228	355	143	278	38	166	314
Sept. 10	280	71	191	316	92	241	2	127	265	50
Sept. 17	19	155	278	58	189	325	88	230	359	135
Sept. 24	105	242	20	152	274	54	191	323	84	225
Oct. 1	193	341	116	237	4	152	287	47	174	324
Oct. 8	291	79	200	324	103	249	11	135	276	58
Oct. 15	27	163	287	68	198	333	98	239	8	143
Oct. 22	113	252	28	162	282	64	199	332	92	235
Oct. 29	201	350	125	245	12	162	295	56	182	334
Nov. 5	302	87	209	333	114	256	19	144	286	66
Nov. 12	36	171	297	76	207	341	109	247	17	150
Nov. 19	121	262	37	171	291	73	208	341	101	244
Nov. 26	209	0	133	254	20	173	303	65	190	345
Dec. 3	312	95	217	342	124	265	27	154	295	75
Dec. 10	45	179	307	84	216	348	119	255	27	158
Dec. 17	129	271	46	180	299	82	218	350	110	252
Dec. 24	217	11	141	263	28	184	311	73	199	355
Dec. 31	321	103	225	352	132	273	35	164	303	84

	1961	1962	1963	1964	1965	1966	1967	1968	1969	1970
Jan. 1	96	217	350	128	266	27	163	298	76	197
Jan. 8	179	315	89	217	350	126	260	27	161	297
Jan. 15	275	54	179	302	86	225	349	112	257	36
Jan. 22	18	141	264	35	189	311	74	207	359	122
Jan. 29	105	225	1	136	275	35	173	306	85	206
Feb. 5	188	323	99	225	360	134	270	35	171	305
Feb. 12	284	64	187	310	95	235	357	121	267	45
Feb. 19	26	150	272	46	197	320	81	218	7	130
Feb. 26	113	234	11	144	283	45	182	315	93	216
Mar. 5	198	331	109	245	9	142	280	54	180	313

	1961	1962	1963	1964	1965	1966	1967	1968	1969	1970
Mar. 12	293	73	195	332	105	244	5	142	277	54
Mar. 19	34	159	280	71	205	329	90	243	15	139
Mar. 26	122	243	19	167	291	54	190	338	101	226
Apr. 2	208	340	119	253	18	151	290	63	189	323
Apr. 9	303	82	204	340	116	252	14	150	288	62
Apr. 16	42	167	288	81	213	337	99	253	23	147
Apr. 23	130	253	28	176	299	64	198	347	109	235
Apr. 30	216	349	128	261	27	161	298	71	197	333
May 7	314	90	213	348	127	260	23	158	299	70
May 14	51	176	298	91	222	345	109	262	32	155
May 21	137	263	36	186	307	74	207	357	117	245
May 28	225	359	137	270	35	172	307	80	205	344
June 4	325	98	222	357	137	268	31	168	309	78
June 11	60	184	308	99	231	353	119	270	42	163
June 18	146	272	45	195	315	82	217	6	126	253
June 25	233	10	145	279	43	183	315	89	214	355
July 2	336	106	230	6	147	276	40	178	318	87
July 9	70	191	318	108	241	1	129	279	51	171
July 16	154	281	56	204	324	91	227	14	135	261
July 23	241	21	153	288	52	193	323	98	223	5
July 30	345	115	238	16	156	286	47	188	327	97
Aug. 6	79	200	327	116	250	10	138	288	60	180
Aug. 13	163	289	66	212	333	99	238	22	144	270
Aug. 20	250	32	161	296	61	203	331	106	233	14
Aug. 27	353	124	246	27	164	295	55	199	335	106
Sept. 3	88	208	336	126	259	19	147	297	68	189
Sept. 10	172	297	77	220	342	108	249	30	152	279
Sept. 17	260	41	170	304	72	212	340	114	244	23
Sept. 24	1	134	254	37	172	304	64	208	344	115
Oct. 1	97	217	344	136	267	28	155	308	76	198
Oct. 8	180	306	88	228	351	117	259	38	161	289
Oct. 15	270	50	179	312	82	220	350	122	254	31
Oct. 22	10	143	262	47	182	313	73	217	353	123
Oct. 29	105	226	352	146	275	37	163	318	84	207
Nov. 5	189	315	97	237	359	127	268	47	168	299
Nov. 12	281	58	188	320	93	228	359	130	264	39
Nov. 19	19	151	271	55	191	321	82	225	3	131
Nov. 26	113	235	1	157	282	45	172	328	92	215

	1961	1962	1963	1964	1965	1966	1967	1968	1969	1970
Dec. 3	197	326	105	245	7	138	276	55	176	310
Dec. 10	291	66	197	328	102	237	7	139	273	48
Dec. 17	30	159	280	63	202	329	91	234	13	139
Dec. 24	121	243	11	167	291	53	183	337	101	223
Dec. 31	204	336	113	254	14	149	284	64	184	320

	1971	1972	1973	1974	1975	1976	1977	1978	1979	1980
Jan. 1	335	109	246	8	147	279	56	179	318	90
Jan. 8	71	197	332	108	243	6	144	278	54	176
Jan. 15	158	283	69	207	328	93	240	18	139	263
Jan. 22	244	20	169	292	54	192	339	102	224	4
Jan. 29	344	117	255	17	156	288	64	188	327	99
Feb. 5	81	204	342	116	253	14	153	287	63	184
Feb. 12	167	291	79	216	337	101	251	26	147	271
Feb. 19	252	31	177	300	62	203	347	110	233	14
Feb. 26	353	126	263	27	164	297	72	199	334	109
Mar. 5	91	224	351	124	262	34	162	296	72	204
Mar. 12	176	312	90	224	346	122	262	34	156	293
Mar. 19	261	55	185	309	72	226	356	118	243	37
Mar. 26	1	149	270	37	172	320	80	208	343	130
Apr. 2	100	233	360	134	270	43	170	307	80	213
Apr. 9	184	320	101	232	355	131	273	42	164	302
Apr. 16	271	64	194	317	82	235	5	126	254	46
Apr. 23	9	158	278	47	181	329	88	217	352	139
Apr. 30	109	242	8	145	278	52	178	318	88	222
May 7	193	329	111	240	3	141	282	50	173	312
May 14	281	73	203	324	92	243	14	134	264	54
May 21	19	167	287	55	191	337	97	226	3	147
May 28	117	251	16	156	286	61	187	328	96	231
June 4	201	339	120	249	11	151	291	59	180	323
June 11	291	81	213	333	102	252	23	143	273	63
June 18	29	176	296	64	201	346	106	234	13	155
June 25	125	260	25	167	295	69	196	338	105	239
July 2	209	349	129	258	19	162	299	68	188	334
July 9	300	90	222	341	111	261	32	152	282	72
July 16	40	184	305	72	212	354	115	243	24	163
July 23	133	268	35	176	303	78	206	347	114	248
July 30	217	0	137	267	27	172	308	77	197	344

	1971	**1972**	**1973**	**1974**	**1975**	**1976**	**1977**	**1978**	**1979**	**1980**
Aug. 6	309	99	230	350	120	271	40	161	290	83
Aug. 13	51	192	314	81	223	2	124	252	34	171
Aug. 20	142	276	45	185	312	86	217	356	123	256
Aug. 27	225	10	146	276	36	182	317	86	206	353
Sept. 3	317	109	238	360	128	281	48	170	299	93
Sept. 10	61	200	322	90	232	10	132	262	43	180
Sept. 17	151	284	56	193	321	94	228	4	132	264
Sept. 24	234	20	155	284	45	191	326	94	215	2
Oct. 1	325	120	246	9	136	291	56	179	308	103
Oct. 8	70	208	330	101	241	19	140	273	51	189
Oct. 15	160	292	66	202	330	102	238	12	140	273
Oct. 22	243	28	165	292	54	199	336	102	225	10
Oct. 29	334	130	254	17	146	301	64	187	318	112
Nov. 5	79	217	338	112	249	27	148	284	59	197
Nov. 12	169	300	76	210	339	111	247	21	148	282
Nov. 19	253	36	175	300	63	207	347	110	234	18
Nov. 26	344	139	262	25	156	310	73	195	329	120
Dec. 3	87	226	346	122	257	36	157	294	67	206
Dec. 10	177	310	84	220	347	121	255	31	156	292
Dec. 17	261	45	185	308	72	216	356	118	242	28
Dec. 24	355	148	271	33	167	318	81	203	340	128
Dec. 31	95	235	355	132	265	44	166	303	76	214

	1981	**1982**	**1983**	**1984**	**1985**	**1986**	**1987**	**1988**	**1989**	**1990**
Jan. 1	226	350	129	260	36	162	300	71	205	333
Jan. 8	315	89	225	346	126	260	36	156	297	72
Jan. 15	53	188	309	73	225	358	119	243	37	168
Jan. 22	149	272	35	176	319	82	206	348	129	252
Jan. 29	234	0	137	270	43	172	308	81	213	343
Feb. 5	324	98	234	354	135	270	44	164	306	82
Feb. 12	64	196	317	81	236	6	128	252	48	175
Feb. 19	157	280	45	185	328	90	217	356	138	260
Feb. 26	242	10	145	279	51	182	316	90	222	353
Mar. 5	332	108	242	15	143	280	52	185	313	93
Mar. 12	74	204	326	104	246	14	136	275	57	184
Mar. 19	166	288	55	208	337	97	227	19	147	268
Mar. 26	250	20	154	300	60	191	326	111	230	1
Apr. 2	340	119	250	24	151	291	60	194	322	103

	1981	1982	1983	1984	1985	1986	1987	1988	1989	1990
Apr. 9	84	212	334	114	255	22	144	286	66	192
Apr. 16	175	296	66	216	346	106	237	27	156	276
Apr. 23	259	28	164	309	69	199	336	119	240	9
Apr. 30	349	130	258	33	160	302	68	203	331	113
May 7	93	221	342	124	264	31	152	297	75	201
May 14	184	304	75	225	355	114	246	36	165	285
May 21	268	36	175	317	78	207	347	127	249	18
May 28	358	140	266	41	170	311	76	211	341	122
June 4	102	230	350	135	272	40	160	307	83	210
June 11	193	313	84	234	3	123	255	45	173	294
June 18	277	45	185	325	87	216	357	135	258	27
June 25	8	149	275	49	180	320	85	219	352	130
July 2	110	239	359	146	281	49	169	317	92	219
July 9	201	322	93	244	11	133	263	55	181	304
July 16	286	54	196	333	96	225	7	143	266	37
July 23	19	158	284	57	191	328	94	227	3	138
July 30	119	248	7	155	290	57	178	327	101	227
Aug. 6	210	331	101	254	19	142	272	66	189	313
Aug. 13	294	64	205	341	104	236	16	152	274	48
Aug. 20	30	166	293	66	202	337	103	236	13	147
Aug. 27	128	256	17	164	299	65	187	335	111	235
Sept. 3	218	340	110	264	27	151	281	75	197	321
Sept. 10	302	75	214	350	112	247	24	160	282	59
Sept. 17	40	174	302	74	212	345	112	245	23	156
Sept. 24	138	264	26	172	309	73	197	343	121	243
Oct. 1	226	349	119	274	36	159	292	84	206	329
Oct. 8	310	86	222	359	120	258	32	169	291	70
Oct. 15	50	183	310	84	220	354	120	255	31	165
Oct. 22	148	272	35	181	319	81	206	352	130	251
Oct. 29	234	357	130	282	44	167	303	92	214	337
Nov. 5	318	96	230	8	129	268	40	178	300	79
Nov. 12	58	193	318	93	229	4	128	265	39	175
Nov. 19	158	280	44	190	329	90	214	2	139	260
Nov. 26	243	5	141	290	53	175	314	100	223	345
Dec. 3	327	106	238	16	139	277	49	185	310	88
Dec. 10	66	203	326	103	237	14	136	274	48	185
Dec. 17	167	288	52	200	337	98	222	12	147	269
Dec. 24	252	13	152	298	62	184	324	108	232	355
Dec. 31	337	114	248	24	149	285	59	193	320	96

	1991	**1992**	**1993**	**1994**	**1995**	**1996**	**1997**	**1998**	**1999**	**2000**
Jan. 1	111	242	15	145	281	53	185	317	92	223
Jan. 8	206	326	108	244	16	136	279	56	186	307
Jan. 15	289	54	210	337	99	225	21	147	270	37
Jan. 22	18	158	299	61	190	329	110	231	2	140
Jan. 29	119	252	23	155	290	62	193	326	101	232
Feb. 5	214	335	116	254	24	145	287	66	193	315
Feb. 12	298	63	220	345	108	235	31	155	278	47
Feb. 19	29	166	308	69	201	337	119	239	12	148
Feb. 26	128	260	32	164	299	70	202	335	111	240
Mar. 5	222	356	124	265	32	166	295	76	201	337
Mar. 12	306	87	229	354	116	259	39	164	285	72
Mar. 19	39	189	317	77	211	360	128	248	22	170
Mar. 26	138	280	41	172	310	90	212	343	121	260
Apr. 2	230	5	133	275	40	175	305	86	210	345
Apr. 9	314	98	237	3	123	270	47	173	294	83
Apr. 16	49	198	326	86	220	9	136	257	31	180
Apr. 23	148	288	50	180	320	98	221	351	132	268
Apr. 30	238	13	143	284	48	183	315	95	218	353
May 7	322	109	245	12	132	281	55	182	302	93
May 14	57	207	335	95	228	18	144	267	39	190
May 21	158	296	59	189	330	106	230	1	141	276
May 28	247	21	154	292	57	191	326	103	227	1
June 4	330	119	253	21	141	291	64	190	311	102
June 11	66	217	343	105	236	28	152	276	48	199
June 18	168	304	68	199	340	114	238	11	150	285
June 25	256	29	165	300	66	199	337	111	236	10
July 2	339	129	262	29	150	300	73	198	321	111
July 9	74	227	351	114	245	38	160	285	57	209
July 16	177	313	76	210	348	123	246	22	158	293
July 23	265	38	175	309	75	208	347	120	245	19
July 30	349	137	272	37	160	308	83	206	331	119
Aug. 6	83	237	359	123	255	48	169	293	67	218
Aug. 13	186	322	84	221	356	132	254	33	166	302
Aug. 20	273	47	185	318	83	218	356	129	253	29
Aug. 27	358	146	282	45	169	317	93	214	340	128
Sept. 3	93	246	7	131	265	56	177	301	78	226
Sept. 10	194	331	92	231	4	141	263	43	174	311
Sept. 17	281	56	194	327	91	228	5	138	261	39

	1991	1992	1993	1994	1995	1996	1997	1998	1999	2000
Sept. 24	8	154	292	53	178	326	102	223	349	137
Oct. 1	104	254	16	139	276	64	186	310	89	234
Oct. 8	202	339	101	241	13	149	273	53	183	319
Oct. 15	289	66	202	337	99	238	13	148	269	49
Oct. 22	16	164	301	61	187	336	111	231	357	148
Oct. 29	115	262	25	148	287	72	195	318	100	242
Nov. 5	211	347	111	250	22	157	283	61	193	326
Nov. 12	297	76	211	346	107	247	22	157	277	58
Nov. 19	24	174	309	70	194	346	119	240	5	159
Nov. 26	126	270	33	156	297	80	203	328	109	251
Dec. 3	220	355	121	258	31	165	293	69	202	334
Dec. 10	305	85	220	355	115	256	31	165	286	67
Dec. 17	32	185	317	79	203	357	127	249	13	169
Dec. 24	135	278	41	166	306	89	211	338	117	260
Dec. 31	230	3	131	266	41	173	303	78	211	343

	2001	2002	2003	2004	2005	2006	2007	2008	2009	2010
Jan. 1	355	128	263	33	165	300	74	203	336	111
Jan. 8	89	228	355	117	260	39	165	288	71	211
Jan. 15	193	317	79	209	4	127	249	20	174	297
Jan. 22	280	41	174	310	91	211	346	121	261	21
Jan. 29	4	137	273	42	175	308	84	211	345	119
Feb. 5	97	238	3	126	268	49	173	296	80	221
Feb. 12	202	326	87	219	12	136	257	31	182	306
Feb. 19	289	49	184	319	99	220	356	130	269	31
Feb. 26	13	145	283	49	184	316	94	219	355	127
Mar. 5	106	248	11	147	278	59	181	317	90	229
Mar. 12	210	334	95	244	20	145	265	56	190	315
Mar. 19	298	58	193	342	107	229	4	153	277	40
Mar. 26	23	153	293	69	193	325	104	239	4	136
Apr. 2	116	257	20	155	289	67	190	325	101	237
Apr. 9	218	343	104	255	28	154	274	67	198	323
Apr. 16	306	68	202	351	115	239	12	162	285	50
Apr. 23	32	162	303	77	202	334	114	247	12	146
Apr. 30	127	265	29	163	300	75	199	333	112	245
May 7	226	352	113	264	37	162	284	76	207	331
May 14	314	77	210	1	123	248	21	172	293	59
May 21	40	173	312	86	210	345	122	256	20	157

	2001	2002	2003	2004	2005	2006	2007	2008	2009	2010
May 28	138	273	38	171	311	83	207	342	123	254
June 4	235	0	122	273	46	170	294	84	217	339
June 11	322	87	219	11	132	257	30	181	302	68
June 18	48	183	320	95	218	356	130	265	29	168
June 25	149	281	46	181	321	92	216	352	132	262
July 2	245	8	132	281	56	178	304	93	227	347
July 9	330	95	229	20	140	266	41	190	310	76
July 16	56	195	328	104	227	7	138	274	38	179
July 23	158	290	54	191	330	101	224	2	140	272
July 30	254	16	142	290	65	186	313	101	236	356
Aug. 6	339	103	239	28	149	274	52	198	319	84
Aug. 13	65	205	336	112	236	17	147	282	47	188
Aug. 20	167	299	62	201	338	110	232	12	149	281
Aug. 27	264	24	151	299	74	194	321	111	245	5
Sept. 3	348	112	250	36	158	282	63	206	328	93
Sept. 10	74	215	345	120	246	26	156	290	58	197
Sept. 17	176	309	70	211	347	120	240	22	157	290
Sept. 24	273	33	159	309	83	203	330	122	253	14
Oct. 1	356	120	261	44	167	291	73	214	336	103
Oct. 8	84	224	354	128	256	34	165	298	68	205
Oct. 15	184	318	78	220	355	129	248	31	167	299
Oct. 22	281	42	167	320	91	212	338	132	261	23
Oct. 29	5	129	271	52	175	301	82	222	344	113
Nov. 5	95	232	4	136	266	42	174	306	78	213
Nov. 12	193	327	87	229	5	137	257	40	177	307
Nov. 19	289	51	176	331	99	221	346	143	268	31
Nov. 26	13	139	280	61	183	312	91	231	352	123
Dec. 3	105	240	13	144	276	51	183	315	87	223
Dec. 10	203	335	96	237	15	145	267	48	188	315
Dec. 17	297	59	185	341	107	229	356	152	277	39
Dec. 24	21	150	288	70	190	322	98	240	0	134
Dec. 31	114	249	22	153	285	60	191	324	96	232

	2011	2012	2013	2014	2015	2016	2017	2018	2019	2020
Jan. 1	246	13	147	281	57	183	318	92	229	352
Jan. 8	335	98	242	22	145	268	54	193	314	78
Jan. 15	59	193	345	108	229	5	155	278	39	178
Jan. 22	158	292	71	192	330	103	241	3	140	274

	2011	2012	2013	2014	2015	2016	2017	2018	2019	2020
Jan. 29	256	21	157	290	67	190	328	101	239	0
Feb. 5	343	106	252	31	153	276	64	201	323	86
Feb. 12	67	204	352	116	237	16	162	287	48	188
Feb. 19	167	301	79	202	338	112	248	13	148	283
Feb. 26	266	29	166	298	77	198	337	110	248	9
Mar. 5	351	127	263	39	162	297	75	209	332	108
Mar. 12	76	229	0	125	247	40	171	295	58	212
Mar. 19	175	324	87	211	346	135	256	23	157	306
Mar. 26	275	49	175	308	86	219	345	120	256	29
Apr. 2	0	135	274	47	171	306	86	217	341	116
Apr. 9	85	238	9	133	256	49	180	303	68	220
Apr. 16	183	333	95	221	354	144	265	32	166	315
Apr. 23	284	57	183	319	94	228	353	131	264	38
Apr. 30	9	144	284	55	179	315	96	226	349	126
May 7	95	247	19	141	267	57	189	310	78	228
May 14	192	343	103	230	4	153	273	40	176	323
May 21	292	66	191	330	102	237	1	142	272	47
May 28	18	153	294	64	187	325	105	235	357	136
June 4	105	255	28	149	276	66	198	319	88	237
June 11	202	352	112	238	15	162	282	49	187	331
June 18	300	75	199	340	110	245	10	152	280	55
June 25	26	163	303	73	195	335	114	244	5	147
July 2	114	263	37	157	286	75	207	327	96	246
July 9	213	360	121	246	25	170	291	57	198	339
July 16	308	84	209	350	119	254	20	161	289	63
July 23	34	174	311	82	203	346	122	253	13	157
July 30	123	273	46	166	294	85	216	336	105	256
Aug. 6	224	8	130	255	36	177	300	66	208	347
Aug. 13	317	92	219	359	128	262	31	170	298	71
Aug. 20	42	184	320	92	211	356	131	262	22	167
Aug. 27	132	283	54	175	302	95	224	345	113	267
Sept. 3	235	16	138	264	46	186	308	76	217	356
Sept. 10	326	100	229	8	137	270	42	178	307	79
Sept. 17	50	194	329	100	220	5	140	270	31	176
Sept. 24	140	293	62	184	311	106	232	354	122	277
Oct. 1	244	24	146	274	55	194	316	87	226	5
Oct. 8	335	108	240	16	146	278	52	186	316	88
Oct. 15	59	202	339	109	229	13	150	278	40	184

	2011	2012	2013	2014	2015	2016	2017	2018	2019	2020
Oct. 22	148	304	70	193	320	116	240	3	131	287
Oct. 29	253	33	154	285	63	203	324	97	234	14
Nov. 5	345	116	250	24	155	287	61	196	324	97
Nov. 12	68	211	349	117	238	21	161	286	49	192
Nov. 19	158	314	78	201	330	125	249	11	142	295
Nov. 26	261	42	162	296	71	212	332	108	242	22
Dec. 3	353	125	258	34	163	296	69	206	332	107
Dec. 10	77	219	359	124	247	30	171	294	57	201
Dec. 17	168	323	87	209	341	133	257	18	153	303
Dec. 24	269	51	171	306	80	221	341	117	251	31
Dec. 31	1	135	266	44	171	306	77	216	340	116

	2021	2022	2023	2024	2025	2026	2027	2028	2029	2030
Jan. 1	129	263	40	162	301	74	211	332	111	246
Jan. 8	226	4	125	248	38	174	295	59	211	343
Jan. 15	324	88	210	350	135	258	21	161	305	68
Jan. 22	50	175	311	85	220	346	122	256	29	158
Jan. 29	139	272	49	170	310	84	220	340	120	256
Feb. 5	237	12	134	256	49	181	304	67	222	351
Feb. 12	333	96	219	359	143	266	31	170	313	76
Feb. 19	58	185	319	94	228	356	130	266	38	167
Feb. 26	147	282	58	179	318	94	228	349	128	266
Mar. 5	248	19	142	278	60	189	312	89	232	359
Mar. 12	341	104	229	22	152	274	41	193	323	83
Mar. 19	66	194	328	116	236	5	139	287	46	176
Mar. 26	155	292	66	200	326	105	236	10	136	277
Apr. 2	258	27	151	288	70	198	320	99	241	8
Apr. 9	351	112	239	30	161	282	51	201	332	92
Apr. 16	74	203	338	125	245	13	150	295	55	184
Apr. 23	163	303	74	208	334	116	244	19	145	287
Apr. 30	267	36	159	298	78	206	328	110	249	17
May 7	0	120	249	39	171	290	61	210	341	100
May 14	83	211	348	133	254	21	160	303	64	192
May 21	172	314	82	217	343	125	252	27	155	296
May 28	276	45	166	309	87	216	336	121	257	26
June 4	9	129	258	48	179	299	69	220	349	109
June 11	92	219	359	141	263	30	171	311	73	201
June 18	182	323	91	225	354	134	261	35	166	305

	2021	2022	2023	2024	2025	2026	2027	2028	2029	2030
June 25	284	54	175	319	95	225	344	131	266	35
July 2	18	138	267	58	187	308	78	230	357	119
July 9	101	228	10	149	272	39	181	319	82	211
July 16	192	332	100	233	4	143	270	43	176	313
July 23	293	63	183	329	104	233	353	140	275	44
July 30	26	147	275	68	195	317	86	240	5	128
Aug. 6	110	237	19	157	280	49	190	327	90	222
Aug. 13	203	341	109	241	15	151	279	51	187	322
Aug. 20	302	72	192	338	114	242	3	149	285	51
Aug. 27	34	156	284	79	203	326	95	250	13	136
Sept. 3	118	248	28	166	288	60	199	336	98	233
Sept. 10	214	349	118	250	25	160	288	60	197	331
Sept. 17	312	80	201	346	124	250	12	157	295	59
Sept. 24	42	165	293	88	211	335	105	259	22	145
Oct. 1	126	259	36	175	296	71	207	345	106	243
Oct. 8	223	358	126	259	34	169	296	70	205	340
Oct. 15	322	88	211	355	134	258	21	166	305	67
Oct. 22	50	173	303	97	220	342	116	268	31	152
Oct. 29	134	269	44	184	304	81	215	354	115	253
Nov. 5	232	7	134	268	43	179	304	80	214	350
Nov. 12	332	96	219	3	144	266	29	175	314	76
Nov. 19	59	181	314	106	229	350	127	276	39	161
Nov. 26	143	279	53	192	313	91	224	2	124	262
Dec. 3	240	17	142	278	51	189	312	89	222	360
Dec. 10	342	104	227	13	153	274	37	186	323	84
Dec. 17	68	189	325	113	238	359	137	284	48	170
Dec. 24	152	288	62	200	323	99	234	10	134	270
Dec 31	248	27	150	287	59	198	320	98	231	9

	2031	2032	2033	2034	2035	2036	2037	2038	2039	2040
Jan. 1	22	142	282	57	192	312	93	229	2	122
Jan. 8	105	229	23	153	275	39	195	323	85	211
Jan. 15	192	333	115	237	4	143	286	47	176	314
Jan. 22	293	67	199	329	104	238	9	140	275	48
Jan. 29	30	151	290	68	200	321	101	240	10	131
Feb. 5	114	237	33	161	284	49	205	331	94	221
Feb. 12	203	341	124	245	14	151	295	55	186	322
Feb. 19	301	76	208	338	113	246	18	149	285	56

	2031	2032	2033	2034	2035	2036	2037	2038	2039	2040
Feb. 26	38	159	298	78	208	330	109	251	17	140
Mar. 5	122	261	43	170	292	73	214	340	101	245
Mar. 12	213	4	133	253	24	174	304	63	196	345
Mar. 19	311	96	217	346	123	266	27	157	295	76
Mar. 26	46	180	307	89	215	350	118	261	26	161
Apr. 2	130	271	51	178	300	84	222	349	109	256
Apr. 9	223	12	142	262	34	183	312	72	205	354
Apr. 16	322	104	226	354	134	274	36	165	306	84
Apr. 23	54	189	317	98	224	359	128	270	34	169
Apr. 30	138	282	59	188	308	94	230	358	118	266
May 7	231	21	151	271	42	192	320	82	213	4
May 14	333	112	235	3	144	282	45	174	316	92
May 21	62	197	327	107	233	7	139	278	43	176
May 28	146	293	68	196	316	104	239	7	127	276
June 4	240	31	159	280	50	202	328	91	221	14
June 11	343	120	243	12	154	291	54	184	325	100
June 18	71	205	338	116	242	15	150	286	52	185
June 25	155	302	77	205	325	114	248	15	136	284
July 2	248	41	167	290	59	213	336	100	231	24
July 9	352	129	252	23	163	299	62	195	333	109
July 16	80	213	349	124	251	23	160	294	61	194
July 23	164	311	86	213	335	122	258	23	146	293
July 30	257	51	175	298	68	223	345	109	240	33
Aug. 6	1	138	260	34	171	308	70	206	341	118
Aug. 13	89	222	359	133	259	32	170	303	69	204
Aug. 20	174	320	96	221	344	131	268	31	155	301
Aug. 27	267	61	183	307	79	232	353	117	251	42
Sept. 3	9	147	268	45	179	317	78	217	350	127
Sept. 10	98	231	8	142	267	42	179	313	77	214
Sept. 17	183	328	107	229	353	139	278	39	164	311
Sept. 24	277	70	192	315	90	240	2	125	262	50
Oct. 1	17	155	276	55	188	325	87	227	359	135
Oct. 8	105	241	16	152	275	52	187	323	85	224
Oct. 15	192	337	116	237	2	149	287	48	172	321
Oct. 22	288	78	201	323	101	248	11	133	273	58
Oct. 29	26	164	286	64	197	333	97	235	8	143
Nov. 5	113	251	24	161	283	62	195	332	93	233
Nov. 12	200	347	125	246	10	160	295	56	180	332

	2031	2032	2033	2034	2035	2036	2037	2038	2039	2040
Nov. 19	299	86	209	331	111	256	19	142	282	66
Nov. 26	35	172	296	72	206	341	107	243	17	151
Dec. 3	121	260	33	171	291	71	205	341	101	241
Dec. 10	207	358	133	255	17	171	303	65	188	343
Dec. 17	309	94	218	341	120	264	27	152	291	75
Dec. 24	45	179	306	80	216	349	117	251	27	159
Dec. 31	130	268	43	179	300	79	215	349	110	249

	2041	2042	2043	2044	2045	2046	2047	2048	2049	2050
Jan. 1	263	41	172	293	74	213	341	103	245	25
Jan. 8	7	133	255	22	178	303	65	194	349	113
Jan. 15	96	217	348	125	267	27	160	295	77	197
Jan. 22	180	311	86	218	350	122	258	28	161	293
Jan. 29	271	52	179	302	83	224	349	112	254	35
Feb. 5	16	142	263	32	187	312	73	205	357	122
Feb. 12	105	225	358	133	276	35	169	304	85	206
Feb. 19	189	319	97	226	359	130	269	35	170	301
Feb. 26	280	62	187	310	92	233	357	120	264	44
Mar. 5	24	150	271	57	195	321	81	230	5	131
Mar. 12	114	234	7	156	284	44	178	327	93	215
Mar. 19	198	328	107	246	8	138	279	55	179	310
Mar. 26	290	71	196	331	102	242	6	140	274	52
Apr. 2	32	159	279	68	203	329	90	240	13	139
Apr. 9	122	243	15	166	292	54	186	337	101	225
Apr. 16	207	336	117	254	17	148	289	63	188	320
Apr. 23	301	80	205	338	113	250	15	148	286	60
Apr. 30	41	168	288	78	211	338	99	249	22	148
May 7	130	252	24	176	300	63	195	347	109	234
May 14	215	346	127	262	25	158	297	72	196	330
May 21	312	88	213	347	124	258	24	157	296	69
May 28	50	176	298	87	221	346	108	258	32	156
June 4	138	262	32	185	308	72	204	356	117	243
June 11	223	357	135	271	33	169	306	81	204	342
June 18	322	96	222	355	134	267	32	166	306	77
June 25	59	184	307	96	230	354	118	266	42	164
July 2	146	270	42	195	316	81	214	5	126	251
July 9	231	8	144	280	42	180	314	90	212	352
July 16	332	105	230	5	144	276	40	176	314	87

	2041	2042	2043	2044	2045	2046	2047	2048	2049	2050
July 23	69	192	317	104	240	2	127	275	51	172
July 30	155	279	52	204	325	89	225	14	135	259
Aug. 6	240	18	152	288	51	190	322	98	222	2
Aug. 13	341	114	238	15	152	285	48	187	323	96
Aug. 20	79	200	326	113	250	10	136	285	60	181
Aug. 27	164	287	64	212	334	97	236	22	144	267
Sept. 3	249	29	160	297	60	200	331	106	231	11
Sept. 10	350	124	246	25	160	295	56	197	331	106
Sept. 17	88	209	334	123	259	19	144	295	69	189
Sept. 24	172	295	74	220	342	106	247	30	152	277
Oct. 1	258	38	169	305	70	208	340	114	242	19
Oct. 8	358	134	254	35	169	304	65	206	341	115
Oct. 15	97	218	342	134	267	28	152	306	76	198
Oct. 22	181	304	85	228	351	115	256	38	161	287
Oct. 29	269	46	179	312	81	217	349	122	252	28
Nov. 5	7	143	263	43	179	313	73	214	351	123
Nov. 12	105	226	350	144	275	37	161	316	84	207
Nov. 19	189	314	94	236	359	125	265	47	168	297
Nov. 26	279	54	188	320	90	225	359	130	261	36
Dec. 3	17	151	272	52	189	321	82	222	1	131
Dec. 10	112	235	359	155	283	45	170	326	92	215
Dec. 17	197	324	102	246	6	136	273	56	176	308
Dec. 24	288	63	197	329	99	234	7	139	270	46
Dec. 31	28	159	281	59	200	329	91	230	12	139

TABLE OF BASE NUMBERS

	Aries (13)	Taurus (14)	Gemini (15)	Cancer (16)	Leo (17)	Virgo (18)	Libra (19)	Scorpio (20)	Sagittarius (21)	Capricorn (22)	Aquarius (23)	Pisces (24)
0 deg.	0	30	60	90	120	150	180	210	240	270	300	330
1 deg.	1	31	61	91	121	151	181	211	241	271	301	331
2 deg.	2	32	62	92	122	152	182	212	242	272	302	332
3 deg.	3	33	63	93	123	153	183	213	243	273	303	333
4 deg.	4	34	64	94	124	154	184	214	244	274	304	334
5 deg.	5	35	65	95	125	155	185	215	245	275	305	335
6 deg.	6	36	66	96	126	156	186	216	246	276	306	336
7 deg.	7	37	67	97	127	157	187	217	247	277	307	337
8 deg.	8	38	68	98	128	158	188	218	248	278	308	338
9 deg.	9	39	69	99	129	159	189	219	249	279	309	339
10 deg.	10	40	70	100	130	160	190	220	250	280	310	340
11 deg.	11	41	71	101	131	161	191	221	251	281	311	341
12 deg.	12	42	72	102	132	162	192	222	252	282	312	342
13 deg.	13	43	73	103	133	163	193	223	253	283	313	343
14 deg.	14	44	74	104	134	164	194	224	254	284	314	344
15 deg.	15	45	75	105	135	165	195	225	255	285	315	345
16 deg.	16	46	76	106	136	166	196	226	256	286	316	346
17 deg.	17	47	77	107	137	167	197	227	257	287	317	347
18 deg.	18	48	78	108	138	168	198	228	258	288	318	248
19 deg.	19	49	79	109	139	169	199	229	259	289	319	349
20 deg.	20	50	80	110	140	170	200	230	260	290	320	350
21 deg.	21	51	81	111	141	171	201	231	261	291	321	351
22 deg.	22	52	82	112	142	172	202	232	262	292	322	352
23 deg.	23	53	83	113	143	173	203	233	263	293	323	353
24 deg.	24	54	84	114	144	174	204	234	264	294	324	354
25 deg.	25	55	85	115	145	175	205	235	265	295	325	355
26 deg.	26	56	86	116	146	176	206	236	266	296	326	356
27 deg.	27	57	87	117	147	177	207	237	267	297	327	357
28 deg.	28	58	88	118	148	178	208	238	268	298	328	358
29 deg.	29	59	89	119	149	179	209	239	269	299	329	359

Glossary

Air. The ancient element representing thought and communication is symbolized by incense and the color yellow. It is associated with the direction of East and its season is spring.

Aquarius. The eleventh sign of the Zodiac. This sign, ruled by Uranus, is a Positive, Fixed, Air sign. It is symbolized by the Water Bearer and is Masculine.

Aries. The first sign of the Zodiac. This sign, ruled by Mars, is a Positive, Cardinal, Fire sign. It is symbolized by the Ram and is Masculine.

Ascendant. Also known as the "Rising Sign," the Ascendant is the first house cusp of the horoscope formed by the degree of the Zodiac "rising" above the eastern horizon at birth. This rising sign has a tremendous effect on an individual's character, appearance, and attitudes.

Aspect. The relationship between planets described as the angle between them as they correspond to their location in the Zodiac. An aspect can also be a relationship between a planet and another angle or important point.

Astrology. The study of the movements of the celestial bodies within our solar system and their relation to the events which occur in our lives.

Autumnal Equinox. Traditionally thought of as September 21, this day is comprised of equal lengths of light and darkness. It is halfway between the summer solstice (longest day of the year) and the winter solstice (shortest day of the year). This day is celebrated as the first day of harvest or the first day of the second harvest.

Balsamic Moon. The phase of the Moon associated with the native's belief in fate. It is the Moon positioned 45 degrees or less behind the Sun in the natal horoscope. In astronomy it is the waning crescent Moon.

Cancer. The fourth sign of the Zodiac. This sign, ruled by the Moon, is a Negative, Cardinal, Water sign. It is symbolized by the Crab and is Feminine.

Capricorn. The tenth sign of the Zodiac. This sign, ruled by Saturn, is a Negative, Cardinal, Earth sign. It is symbolized by the Goat and is Feminine.

Cardinal Signs. The signs falling naturally at the four cardinal points (directions) east, south, west, and north. The Cardinal signs, Aries, Cancer, Libra, and Capricorn focus on initiatory, active, and dynamic qualities.

Conjunction. The angular relationship, or aspect, that exists between two planets in close proximity to each other within the Zodiac.

Crescent Moon. The waxing crescent Moon is the first crescent after the new Moon, halfway to the first quarter. It is the Moon which precedes the natal Sun by 45 degrees or less.

Dark Moon. The phase of the Moon which is conjunct with the Sun, between the balsamic Moon and the new Moon. It is the three days in which the Moon is aligned close enough to the Sun to remain unseen.

Disseminating Moon. The phase of the Moon, also known as the waning gibbous Moon, which is the first 45 degrees of the waning Moon after the full Moon.

Earth. The ancient element representing Nature and money is symbolized by the pentagram, salt, and the color green. It is associated with the direction of North and its season is winter.

Feminine Signs. The Earth and Water signs so designated by their traits of receptivity and passivity. "Feminine" is not in reference to sexual traits or gender.

Fire. The ancient element representing action and change is symbolized by the sacred flame and the color red. It is associated with the direction of South and its season is summer.

Fixed Signs. Taurus, Leo, Scorpio, and Aquarius are associated with a fixed or stable means of self-expression.

Full Moon. The phase of the Moon in opposition to the Sun, or 180 degrees ahead of the Sun. It is the third quarter Moon, and signals the end of its waxing as well as the beginning of its waning.

Gemini. The third sign of the Zodiac. This sign, ruled by Mercury, is a Positive, Mutable, Air sign. It is symbolized by the Twins and is Masculine.

Gibbous Moon. The waxing gibbous Moon in the natal chart is indicative of the need to analyze the self. It is the last 45 degrees of the Moon before the full Moon, or the phase of the Moon which is 135 to 180 degrees in front of the natal Sun.

Leo. The fifth sign of the Zodiac. This sign, ruled by Sun, is a Positive, Fixed, Fire sign. It is symbolized by the Lion and is Masculine.

Libra. The seventh sign of the Zodiac. This sign, ruled by Venus, is a Positive, Cardinal, Air sign. It is symbolized by the Scales and is Masculine.

Masculine Signs. The Fire and Air signs so designated by their reference to aggressiveness. "Masculine" does not refer to sexual traits or gender.

Metonic Cycle. The Metonic cycle pertains to the Moon's position on the horizon at its rising and setting. The Moon appears to rise and set at differing spots along the horizon. The entire cycle, from its rising and setting at the northerly and southerly extremes, known as the major standstills, to its rising and setting at the midway points on the horizon, known as the minor standstills, and back again takes a little over eighteen and one-half years. This cycle accounts for the Moon's trajectory across the sky being a little different every year. Major standstills and minor standstills are the end points and middle points, respectively, in the Metonic cycle. The Greeks, in the fifth century B.C.E., calculated the length of Moon's Metonic cycle to be 235 lunations, approximately nineteen years. These calculations were revised by Callippus, a Greek astronomer, one hundred years later. He calculated the Metonic cycle to be seventy-six years in length. Modern astronomers have calculated the Metonic cycle at 18.61 years. This makes Callippus' calculations in error by one day every 553 years.

Mutable Signs. Flexibility and adaptability are the traits of Gemini, Virgo, Sagittarius, and Pisces.

Negative Sign. Designates the Earth and Water signs as they are related to the "Feminine" traits of passivity and receptivity.

New Moon. The first quarter of the Moon and it begins the lunation cycle. Astrologically, the Moon is conjunct with the Sun.

Node. Most often used in reference to the Moon, but it applies to all planets and the point at which their orbits cross the ecliptic.

Pagan. A Latin term for the people who lived in the country and worshiped the Goddesses and Gods associated with Nature.

Perigee. The point in another planet's orbit where it is closest to the earth.

Phases of the Moon. Particular points within the lunation cycle marking the predetermined stages of the Moon's appearance.

Pisces. The twelfth sign of the Zodiac. This sign, ruled by Neptune, is a Negative, Mutable, Water sign. It is symbolized by two Fish swimming in opposite directions and is Feminine.

Positive Signs. Also called "Masculine" signs, the Fire and Air signs embody assertive, dynamic, and outgoing traits.

Retrograde. The apparent backward motion of a planet when viewed from Earth. The planet appears to reverse its usual course and move backwards. All of the visible planets were observed to change their speed and direction along the ecliptic on a regular basis. The planets appear to slow their normal eastward journey, stop, and reverse their direction, seeming to head west for a short period of time. Each planet has its own retrograde cycle, different from the retrograde cycles of all other planets, and the retrograde motion of a single planet will vary through each cycle. Other than Mercury, Venus, Mars, Jupiter, Saturn, Uranus, Neptune, Pluto, and the asteroids, there are no celestial bodies that exhibit retrograde motion.

Sagittarius. The ninth sign of the Zodiac. This sign, ruled by Jupiter, is a Positive, Mutable, Fire sign. It is symbolized by the Centaur (half man, half horse) and is Masculine.

Scorpio. The eighth sign of the Zodiac. This sign, ruled by Mars and Pluto, is a Negative, Fixed, Water sign. It is symbolized by the Scorpion and is Feminine.

Shields. A form of magical protection. The practitioner visualizes being enclosed in a bubble of white light through which only good can pass.

Spring Equinox. Traditionally thought of as March 21, this day is comprised of equal lengths of light and darkness. It is halfway between the winter solstice (shortest day of the year) and the summer solstice (longest day of the year). This day is celebrated as the first day of spring and the beginning of a new astrological year.

Summer Solstice. The longest day of the year, and the first day of summer. Astrologically, the summer solstice is the time when the Sun reaches its most northern point on the ecliptic, 0 degrees Cancer.

Taurus. The second sign of the Zodiac. This sign, ruled by Venus, is a Negative, Fixed, Earth sign. It is symbolized by the Bull and is Feminine.

Vernal Equinox. Another name for the spring equinox.

Virgo. The sixth sign of the Zodiac. This sign, ruled by Mercury, is a Negative, Mutable, Earth sign. It is symbolized by the Virgin and is Feminine.

Void of Course Moon. The Moon after it has moved away from its last major aspect and before it moves into the next sign. It associated with the lack of action or direction.

Waning. The portion of the lunation cycle from the full Moon to the new Moon in which the visible portion of the Moon decreases in size.

Water. The ancient element representing emotions, sensitivity, and psychic receptivity is symbolized by the chalice and the color blue. It is associated with the direction of West and its season is autumn.

Waxing. The portion of the lunation cycle from the new Moon to the full Moon in which the visible portion of the Moon increases in size.

Winter Solstice. The shortest day of the year, and the first day of winter. Astrologically, the winter solstice is the time when the Sun reaches its most southern point on the ecliptic, 0 degrees Capricorn.

Zodiac. A circle of twelve signs, each representing an equal division of the Zodiac and one of the constellations: Aries, Taurus, Gemini, Cancer, Leo, Virgo, Libra, Scorpio, Sagittarius, Capricorn, Aquarius, and Pisces.

Select Bibliography

Adler, Margot. *Drawing Down the Moon.* Boston: Beacon Press, 1979.

Brueton, Diana. *Many Moons.* New York: Prentice Hall Press, 1991.

Busteed, Marilyn, Richard Tiffany, and Dorothy Wergin. *Phases of the Moon.* Berkeley: Shambhala Publications, 1974.

Campanelli, Pauline. *Ancient Ways.* St. Paul: Llewellyn Publications, 1992.

———. *Wheel of the Year.* St. Paul: Llewellyn Publications, 1990.

Cott, Jonathon. *Isis and Osiris.* New York: Doubleday, 1994.

Cunningham, Scott. *Wicca: A Guide for the Solitary Practitioner.* St. Paul: Llewellyn Publications, 1989.

Farrar, Janet and Stewart Farrar. *A Witches Bible Compleat.* New York: Magickal Childe Publishing, 1984.

Frazer, James G. *The Golden Bough.* Vols. 1 and 2. New York: Gramercy Books, 1993.

George, Demetra. *Mysteries of the Dark Moon.* San Francisco: HarperCollins, 1992.

Giller, Robert M., M.D., and Kathy Matthews. *Natural Prescriptions.* New York: Carol Southern Books, 1994.

Golder, Carol. *Moon Signs for Lovers.* New York: Henry Holt and Company, 1992.

Graves, Robert. *New Larousse Encyclopedia of Mythology.* London: Prometheus Press, 1968.

Hand, Robert. *Essays on Astrology.* Atglen: Whitford Press, 1982.

Hodgson, Joan. *Planetary Harmonies.* Liss, England: White Eagle Publishing Trust, 1980.

Leek, Sybil. *Moon Signs Lunar Astrology.* New York: Berkeley Publishing, 1977.

Lewi, Grant. *Astrology for the Millions.* St. Paul: Llewellyn Publications, 1990.

Lineman, Rose and Jan Popelka. *Compendium of Astrology.* Gloucester: Para Research, 1984.

Llewellyn's 1994 Organic Gardening Almanac. St. Paul: Llewellyn Publications, 1993.

Llewellyn's 1995 Moon Sign Book. St. Paul: Llewellyn Publications, 1994.

Llewellyn's 1996 Magical Almanac. St. Paul: Llewellyn Publications, 1995.

Llewellyn's Astrological Calendar 1996. St. Paul: Llewellyn Publications, 1995.

MacGregor, Geddes. *Dictionary of Religion and Philosophy.* New York, Paragon House, 1989.

Puharich, A. *Beyond Telepathy.* London: Darton, Longman, and Todd, 1962.

Sakioan, Frances and Louis S. Acker. *The Astrologer's Handbook.* New York: Harper Row, 1973.

Shadwynn. *The Crafted Cup.* St. Paul: Llewellyn Publications, 1994.

Townley, John. *Astrological Life Cycles: A Planetary Guide to Personal and Career Opportunities.* Rochester: Destiny Books, 1980.

Valiente, Doreen. *Natural Magic.* Custer: Phoenix Publishing, 1975.

———. *Witchcraft for Tomorrow.* London: Robert Hale, 1985.

Valiente, Doreen and Evan John Jones. *Witchcraft: A Traditional Renewed.* Custer: Phoenix Publishing, 1990.

Walker, Barbara, G. *The Women's Encyclopedia of Myths and Secrets.* San Francisco: HarperCollins, 1983.

Watson, Lyall. *Supernature.* London: Hodder and Stoughton, 1974.

Whitcomb, Bill. *The Magician's Companion.* St. Paul: Llewellyn Publications, 1993.

Zeilik, Michael. *Astronomy: The Evolving Universe.* New York: Harper Row, 1979.

Index

A

B

S

T

U

V

W

Z

LOOK FOR THE CRESCENT MOON

Llewellyn publishes hundreds of books on your favorite subjects! To get these exciting books, including the ones on the following pages, check your local bookstore or order them directly from Llewellyn.

ORDER BY PHONE

- Call toll-free within the U.S. and Canada, 1–800–THE MOON
- In Minnesota, call (651) 291–1970
- We accept VISA, MasterCard, and American Express

ORDER BY MAIL

- Send the full price of your order (MN residents add 7% sales tax) in U.S. funds, plus postage & handling to:

  Llewellyn Worldwide
  P.O. Box 64383, Dept. K521–5
  St. Paul, MN 55164–0383, U.S.A.

POSTAGE & HANDLING

(For the U.S., Canada, and Mexico)

- $4 for orders $15 and under
- $5 for orders over $15
- No charge for orders over $100

We ship UPS in the continental United States. We ship standard mail to P.O. boxes. Orders shipped to Alaska, Hawaii, the Virgin Islands, and Puerto Rico are sent first-class mail. Orders shipped to Canada and Mexico are sent surface mail.

International orders: Airmail—add freight equal to price of each book to the total price of order, plus $5.00 for each non-book item (audio tapes, etc.).

Surface mail—Add $1.00 per item.

Allow 4–6 weeks for delivery on all orders.
Postage and handling rates subject to change.

DISCOUNTS

We offer a 20% discount to group leaders or agents. You must order a minimum of 5 copies of the same book to get our special quantity price.

FREE CATALOG

Get a free copy of our color catalog, *New Worlds of Mind and Spirit.* Subscribe for just $10.00 in the United States and Canada ($30.00 overseas, airmail). Many bookstores carry *New Worlds*—ask for it!

Visit our website at www.llewellyn.com for more information.

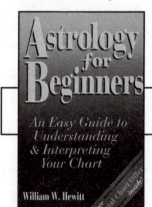

Astrology for the Millions

Grant Lewi

First published in 1940, this practical, do-it-yourself textbook has become a classic guide to computing accurate horoscopes quickly. Throughout the years, it has been improved upon since Grant Lewi's death by his astrological proteges and Llewellyn's expert editors. Grant Lewi is astrology's forerunner to the computer, a man who literally brought astrology to everyone. This, the first new edition since 1979, presents updated transits and new, user-friendly tables to the year 2050, including a new Sun ephemeris of revolutionary simplicity. It's actually easier to use than a computer! Also added is new information on Pluto and rising signs, and a new foreword by Carl Llewellyn Weschcke and introduction by J. Gordon Melton.

Of course, the original material is still here in Lewi's captivating writing style—all of his insights on transits as a tool for planning the future and making the right decisions. His historical analysis of U.S. presidents has been brought up to date to include George Bush. This new edition also features a special *In Memoriam* to Lewi that presents his birth chart.

One of the most remarkable astrology books available, *Astrology for the Millions* allows the reader to cast a personal horoscope in 15 minutes, interpret from the readings and project the horoscope into the future to forecast coming planetary influences and develop "a grand strategy for living."

0-87542-438-4, 6 x 9, 464 pp., tables, charts, soft cover $14.95

To order, call 1–800–THE MOON
Prices subject to change without notice.

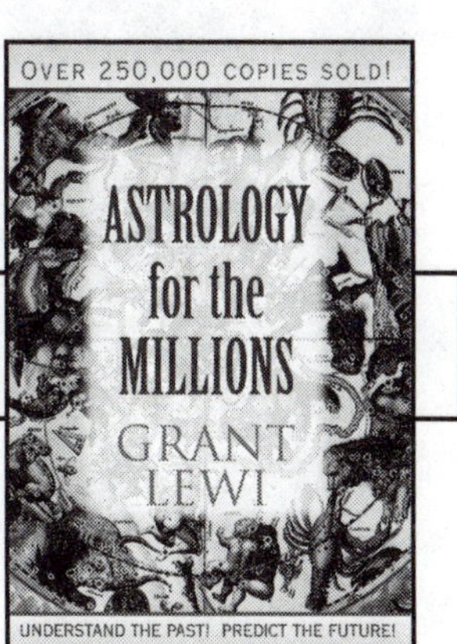

Instant Horoscope Predictor

Find Your Future Fast

Julia Lupton Skalka

Want to know if the planets will smile favorably upon your wedding day? Wondering when to move ahead on that new business venture? Perhaps you're curious as to why you've been so accident prone lately. It's time to look at your transits.

Transits define the relationship between where the planets are today with where they were when you were born. They are an invaluable aid for timing your actions and making decisions. With a copy of your transit chart (easily available from any astrological computing service) and the book *Instant Horoscope Predictor*, you can now discover what's in store for today, next month, even a year from now. Julia Lupton Skalka delivers an easy-to-use guide that will decipher the symbols on your transit chart into clear, usable predictions. In addition, she provides chapters on astrological history, mythology, and transit analyses of four famous people: Grace Kelly, Mata Hari, Theodore Roosevelt and Ted Bundy.

1-56718-668-8, 6 x 9, 464 pp., soft cover **$14.95**

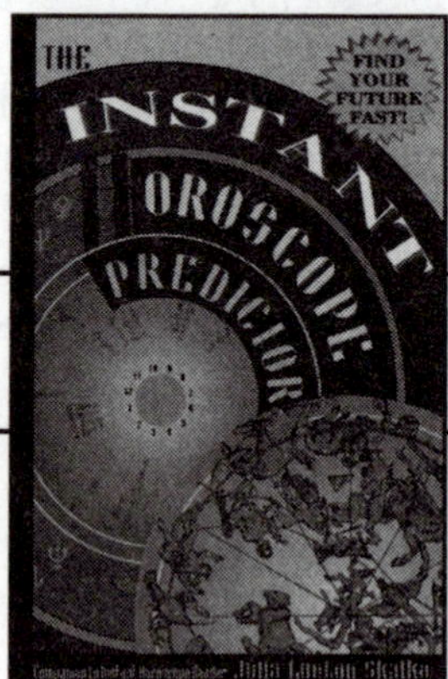

To order, call 1–800–THE MOON

Prices subject to change without notice.

Annette Hinshaw
Earth Time Moon Time

Your map to the future is a *TimeLine Transit/ Progression Forecast.*

Love, money, health—everybody wants to know what lies ahead, and this report will keep you one-up on your future. The *TimeLine* forecast is invaluable for seizing opportunities and timing your moves. This astrological report is completely tailored to you—a unique individual with a unique relation to the cosmos. Reports begin the first day of the month you specify.

APS03-526 3-month report $12.00
APS03-527 6-month report $20.00
APS03-528 12-month report $30.00

Stop looking for love in all the wrong places with *Friends and Lovers.*

Why can't we all just get along? Well, sometimes we can and sometimes we can't, and astrology can shed a lot of light on what makes the difference when you start with a custom-made report like *Friends and Lovers.* Go way beyond "does Capricorn get along with Sagittarius?" Find out how you relate to others, and whether you are really compatible with your current or potential lover, spouse, friend, or business partner! This service includes planetary placements for both people, so send birth data for both and specify "friends" or "lovers."

APS03-529 $20.00

Find out if you and your lover are truly matched with *Sympaticos.*

You have a chart, and your love partner has a chart, but did you know that your relationship has a chart, too? It does—the Composite Chart—a blend of the birth charts of two people, and the method behind this amazingly insightful new report. With *Sympaticos,* you will find out the real secrets of what exists between you, and the essence of what you can do and be together. Be sure to include birth data for both people.

APS03-533 $20.00

Give your child a jump on life with *Child*Star.*

We all want the best for our children, and a large part of that comes from understanding who they are and where their latent talents and challenges lie. Every parent knows that each child enters the world with a unique, distinct personality, and astrology can reveal the forces behind that fresh new face. Written by an astrologer who is also a Montessori© instructor, *Child*Star* is an astrological look at your child's inner world through a skillful interpretation of his or her unique birth chart, and is as relevant for teens as it is for newborns. Specify your child's sex.

APS03-530 $20.00

Now you can take this job and love it with *Opportunities.*

Your career is more than just a job—it's where the real you meets the real world. If you want to know just what the best fit might be, you need this enlightening and detailed report. Your unique talents are needed by someone out there, and by fulfilling that need you will not only be contributing to the world, but to your soul's growth as well. With the right livelihood, you could actually begin to look forward to Mondays!

APS03-534 $20.00

Astrological Services Order Form

Report name and number:

____

Provide the following data on all persons receiving a report:
1st Person's Full Name, including current middle and last name(s):

____

Birth time:__________________ a.m. p.m. (please circle)
Month:__________________ Day:_________ Year:_________
Birthplace (city, county, state, country):

____

____

2nd Person's Full Name (if ordering for more than one person):

____

Birth time:__________________ a.m. p.m. (please circle)
Month:__________________ Day:_________ Year:_________
Birthplace (city, county, state, country):

____

____

Check your birth certificate for the most accurate information.

Billing Information

Please Print

Full Name:______________________________________
Mailing Address:_________________________________
City, State, Zip:_________________________________
Make check or money order payable to Llewellyn Publications, or charge it!
Circle one: Visa MasterCard American Express
Acct.
No.:____
Exp. Date __________
Cardholder Signature

____

Mail this form and payment to: Llewellyn Publications, Computerized Astrological Services, P.O. Box 64383-K521-5, St. Paul, MN 55164.

Allow 4-6 weeks for delivery.

For Readers of

Moon Wise

only

FREE Natal Chart Offer

Thank you for purchasing *Moon Wise*. There are a number of ways to construct a chart wheel. The easiest way, of course, is by computer, and that's why we are giving you this one-time offer of a free natal chart. This extremely accurate chart will provide you with a great deal of information about yourself. Once you receive a chart from us, *Moon Wise* will provide everything you need to know to interpret your Moon sign.

Also, by ordering your free chart, you will be enrolled in Llewellyn's Birthday Club! From now on, you can get any of Llewellyn's astrology reports for 25% off when you order within one month of your birthday! Just write "Birthday Club" on your order form when you order any of the great reports included here, or mention it when ordering by phone. As if that wasn't enough, we will mail you a FREE copy of our fresh new book *What Astrology Can Do for You*! Go for it!

Complete this form with your accurate birth data and mail it to us today. Enjoy your adventure in self-discovery through astrology!

Do not photocopy this form. Only this original will be accepted.

Please Print

Full Name:____

Mailing Address:____________________________________

City, State, Zip:_____________________________________

Birth time:________________ a.m. p.m. (please circle)

Month:________________ Day:________ Year:________

Birthplace (city, county, state, country):

____

____

Check your birth certificate for the most accurate information.

Complete and mail this form to: Llewellyn Publications, Special Chart Offer, P.O. Box 64383-K521-5, St. Paul, MN 55164.

Allow 4-6 weeks for delivery.